Keely

My Life-Changer

To my best neighbors ever! enjoy the journey!

Claudette

Claudette B. Price

with

Eva C. Maddox

Keely

My Life-Changer

All Scripture references in this book are from the
New International Version of the Bible.

Cover design by:
Ben Patterson: www.ourcozyhome.net
and
Candy Abbott: www.fruitbearer.com

WE Ink Publications, Seaford, Delaware
www.WEInk.homestead.com

Why I wanted to share my story . . .

For years I've wanted to share the story of my life with Keely, for it is a real story full of loss and failure, hope and triumph. It is a story that I pray will encourage you as you struggle with the challenges in your own life.

What we become as adults is due partly to our inborn personalities and partly to what we experience growing up. God developed my gift of mercy by enabling me to feel others' pain and trying even as a child, to make it better. Little did I know then that He was preparing me for a lifetime of trying to help others, especially my daughter's.

Only those who have a mentally challenged child can fully understand the depth of heartache and despair that comes upon you with the diagnosis. Dreams shatter, hope dims and life turns upside down. A retarded child will change your life. Keely changed mine.

I became a Christian at age 26 and began to study, pray and seek God's Word for answers. He gave me Philippians 4:13 "I can do all things through Christ who strengthens me" as my life verse. It is only because of His strengthening power that I have been able to care for Keely for over 50 years. He enabled me to understand Keely and to accept her as a special blessing. He taught me how to love unconditionally, the kind of love God has for me; how to find joy in the midst of trials, for I had many; contentment with limited creature comforts; patience when I longed to run ahead and peace in spite of disappointments, illnesses and need.

If you are a care-giver, be patient and kind. Don't try to change the one needing care, pray for God to change you. I couldn't change Keely no matter how hard I tried, but God changed me.

Who helped me tell my story . . .

Through the years, I kept copious notes, hoping that one day I could find someone who would help me write my book, for I am not a writer. I broached the subject with a number of people, but was unsuccessful in enlisting anyone who had the expertise and time to devote to it.

When Eva Maddox, my dear friend for the past 30 years, took up writing as a profession in 2003, I once again began thinking about the book I had been mentally writing for some time. Eva began having a number of articles and stories accepted for publication and I wondered if she might be interested in writing my book. When I asked her, she readily agreed.

Almost immediately I began having doubts. Because we were as close as sisters, would we argue like sisters sometimes do? Would she allow me freedom of expression without insisting I use her words? I prayed for peace and trusted that God would help us to work together in harmony. This book is the result.

Writing this book was a heart-wrenching experience for as I recounted each part of the story to Eva, it was like I was living it all over again. Eva took my words and notes and shaped them into a story that I feel describes my life perfectly. I am blessed by her friendship and her dedication to this project.

Who I want to thank . . .

- First, Keely Ann Price, my special love
- Next, Eva Maddox. Great job!
- Crosspoint Baptist Church family for their love and prayers
- Kevan, my son who lived my story with me
- Wilma Caraway, Eva's friend who spent hours editing this book
- Ben Patterson, and Candy Abbott for their combined efforts in creating my book cover
- Heather Davis, Keely's social worker and devoted friend
- Ken Crest Services for their ongoing help in providing care-givers for Keely
- Leslie Osimo, Keely's private nurse
- Drs. Lori Rousche, David Rilling, David Altman and David Bayard
- Grand View Hospital Radiology Department
- Grand View Transport, I couldn't have done it without you

Please Note . . .

Throughout my book you will see the word "retarded" used. Fifty years ago, this was the term commonly used to describe mentally challenged or learning disabled children and the one I have grown accustomed to. "Retarded" simply means a child's development is slow. It is not a slur unless someone chooses to use it in that way.

Chapter One

Loss and Hope

I squeezed a bit of eye salve into Keely's sightless right eye, wiped the endless drool from her chin, checked her feeding tube and changed her diaper. Finally, she was ready for bed.

As I hoisted her 160-pound frame into the hospital bed, she began her usual repetitive grunts and finger-biting, letting me know she wanted music. I switched on the radio by her bed and watched pleasure sweep across her face. One final pillow adjustment, one slobbery kiss and another day with my daughter had ended. I pulled up the side rail and lingered for a few minutes as her eyes closed in peaceful slumber.

Peace . . . Peace did not describe my life with Keely—quite the opposite.

I was one of five children. There were four girls —Gail, the oldest; Paulette, my twin; and Dolores. Johnny, our brother, was the youngest.

We lived with our maternal grandparents for a few years until our mother became ill and passed away. I was four years old. Although I have vague recollections of the warmth of my mother's presence, I have no concrete memories of her.

My parents, Harvey and Anna Bossert

Our dad was left with five small children to care for so he took us to live with his mother and sister.

Daddy with the five of us

Altogether there was a household of eight—a huge undertaking for our aging Grandmother Bossert and Aunt Margaret.

For some time after we moved in with Grammy Bossert, I remember Daddy coming home from work and going upstairs to his bedroom. He was not the same daddy. Even as a little girl, I recognized his sadness.

Sometimes I would sneak upstairs and lie beside him in the bed. It was my way of comforting my dad. We didn't really talk, but after a little while, he would say, "Go on downstairs, Claudie, I'll be there soon."

Aunt Margaret

Grammy took care of the five of us while Aunt Margaret was working. She dressed and fed us every morning, watched us, did loads of washing and ironing, a big burden on our grandmother. Sometimes she would pile us all on her lap and rock us in her big old rocking chair. I loved Grammy, but I adored Aunt Margaret.

Aunt Margaret's return home from work every day was the moment I waited for. She showered us with love for the years we lived there. She was affectionate, patient and compassionate. Every night she would get us ready for bed, then line us up and read the Bible to us and pray with us.

Aunt Margaret and Grammy took us to Sunday School every Sunday. I was fascinated by the stories of Jesus. His love for children reminded me of the way Aunt Margaret and Grammy loved us.

One day our father announced that we were getting a new mother and her name was Beulah. The words felt like ice my sister Paulette (Polly) once slipped down my shirt.

I didn't want a stepmother. After all, things were fine the way they were.

Aunt Margaret began telling us that Beulah would be a good mother for us and would take care of us. "She will make a good home for you, Claudie, you'll see."

So after a while, I began thinking that maybe this was a good thing.

Daddy and Beulah were married and we four girls went to live with them. Johnny, still very young, was not permitted to come with us. Beulah insisted she could not care for a small child. Even at the tender age of seven, my heart burst with pain the day we left our baby brother.

Grammy Bossert

Chapter Two

A New Home

When we moved in with Daddy and Beulah, my hope of having a real mom, vanished rather quickly.

Daddy insisted we call Beulah "mother," and we did. But from the start, the word did not come easily. I was miserable from the start, and I missed Grammy and Aunt Margaret terribly. I called Aunt Margaret whenever I got a chance and she would encourage me to be good and obey Beulah, and would always say that she loved me. "God will be with you, Claudie, no matter what" was her answer whenever I complained of the way things were happening at home.

Our dad had always been affectionate with us, hugging and kissing us goodnight, but shortly after marrying Beulah, she announced, "There would be no more of that." How I resented her and how I missed my dad's loving touch.

Beulah and my dad had three children of their own—Ruby, Phillip and Michael. When Aunt Margaret and Grammy Bossert could no longer care for Johnny, he had to come and live with us too. There were then ten of us in the house.

Beulah's resentment toward Johnny was obvious from the start. She did not permit him to eat with us at the table, but forced him to sit alone and eat, even having a different dish. I remember purposely giving him a dish like the rest of us on more than one occasion and having Beulah yell at me. When we had chicken for dinner, Johnny was only allowed one wing. If I could, I would stuff another piece of chicken in my pocket or a piece of bread and sneak it to him. My heart ached for my little brother and helping him was worth risking Beulah's shrill screams.

Johnny suffered with earaches from time to time and, of course, there were no doctor visits. Sometimes when his ear hurt, I would sneak into his room, sit by his bed and try to soothe him.

"It'll be all right, Johnny," I would say, rubbing his back and stoking his head.

I loved my new little brothers and sister. Beulah would often let them cry until they cried themselves to sleep. I had become an expert at sneaking —always sneaking something to help someone. Several times I sneaked on my hands and knees, behind Beulah's chair, where she often sat reading, to pat baby Ruby on her back until she finally stopped crying and drifted off.

Rarely were there doctor or dental visits. I remember once having a bad toothache for so long that I was desperate. Every time I would tell Daddy, he would tell me to put an aspirin on it. I was sick to death of aspirin and they didn't help anyway. When I could stand the pain no longer, I grabbed Beulah's scissors from her sewing machine on my way up to bed one night and laid them on my nightstand. After I thought everyone was asleep, I slipped out of bed, took the scissors and tiptoed to the bathroom. I leaned over the sink in the dark (for we weren't allowed to turn on the light) and dug out the molar with the scissors. I bled some, but the pain relief was almost immediate. By some miracle, I never got an infection and I never told Daddy or Beulah; neither did they ask about my toothache.

My sister, Dolores, was ill for some time with severe abdominal pain. Beulah insisted she walk several blocks to the doctor's office. I still remember watching her walk down the street, bent over with pain. Hot anger raged through me and I desperately wanted to rescue my little sister. The phone rang shortly after Dolores saw the doctor who informed Beulah to come and take Dolores to the hospital for she had severe appendicitis.

Beulah appeared to be incapable of showing us love and approval, and yet I continually sought it. I wanted her to say I was pretty or did a good job at something, but it never happened. I remember bringing home my 5th grade picture and showing it to her.

"I look terrible," I said, hoping she would disagree.

"Well, pictures don't lie," was her reply. I hid the picture.

Beulah was quick to tell me that my nose was big like my dad's. Well into adulthood, I felt horrible about my nose, trying to shield it with my hand when I felt someone's eyes on me.

Our yard had no trees and so when we went out to play, it was hot and we would get thirsty.

Five Little Bosserts

Beulah would lock the door so that we wouldn't be running in and out. I remember once sneaking in through a basement door, finding a fruit jar and filling it with water so we could have a drink. Apparently Beulah heard the squeal of the pipe and the water running, so we got a good yelling for that, and from then on she locked the basement door.

Beulah always had jobs for us to do. That was okay, but I wanted to hear her say, "Thank you, or good job!" so badly. I never remember hearing those words. Daddy often had me helping him with outside work. I can remember lugging cement blocks, pushing a wheelbarrow full of dirt and mowing the grass with a push mower in the summer heat. I would work until I felt like I would pass out.

When Ruby was a baby, Beulah would often take her for a walk in the stroller and leave us behind. Gail and I decided one day to make a mustard sandwich. We slipped into the kitchen, got out the mustard and bread and proceeded to make our snack and were caught red-handed when Beulah appeared!

"What do you think you are doing!" she shouted. "Get this mess cleaned up!" Of course we were scared like two little puppies being scolded. I no longer remember our punishment, but we were always being punished for something.

Sometimes Daddy would come out and play baseball with us. He had a way of making it exciting. It never lasted long, though, because Beulah would be yelling for him to come in. He always promised he would come back, but he never did.

"You can take your kids and get out of my house!" was one thing I remember Beulah yelling at Daddy when they would have one of their fights. I wished he would take us and get out.

When I was in the 7th grade I got a job working at a local restaurant from five to eleven every weeknight. I was never allowed to participate in any school activities because I had to run home and go immediately to work. Even though I was not allowed to keep my pay, I was happy to be out of the house.

Once I walked by Daddy and Beulah's bedroom and I heard Beulah talking to Daddy. She said, "Claudie, she's the one to watch. She'll be the one to give us trouble." I was devasted. *Why did she say that?* I swallowed the lump in my throat and headed angrily up the stairs. *Maybe I should just give her trouble, if that's what she thinks of me.*

With the hours I worked, I seldom had time for homework, often resorting to copying a friend's work. My education suffered and I quit school after the 10th grade. I felt defeated, frustrated and angry. However, the Claudette everyone saw was a smiling, happy-go-lucky girl, intent on making everyone around her laugh.

Beulah died many years ago and I regret that while she was still living, I was not able to fully appreciate what she gave up when she took the five of us into her life. As a single woman with no children, to be immediately saddled with five kids, then three more within a short space of time, must have been overwhelming to say the least. She was not prepared for such a task and I'm sure she did the best she could do. Nevertheless, as a child growing up in that environment, I saw and felt through the eyes of a child. I was convinced that my stepmother did not love me, I was afraid of her and I couldn't wait to get away.

Beulah and Daddy

Chapter Three

A Perfect Family

While working at the restaurant, I dated several guys, but when I met Willard Price at my sister's wedding, I was smitten. Willard was very good looking, was a hard worker, and one thing very important to me at the time—he owned a brand new car!

He asked me out and I was more than happy to date him. Willard began coming to the restaurant a few minutes before closing at 11 p.m. and driving me home. Usually, he would come in and we would sit on the sofa and watch television. On weekends we would take in a movie, something I had rarely been able to do, so it was exciting for me. Willard was certainly not a talker and that bothered me some, but I dismissed it as trivial. So we continued to date and then one day he popped the question. By then I knew there were things about him that troubled me, but I turned a blind eye to them and agreed to marriage. I was about as ready for marriage as Beulah was ready to take on five kids.

We drove to New York City for a weekend honeymoon, and spent two days walking around the area of our hotel and eating at nearby restaurants. Since I was unsuccessful at interesting Willard in conversation, I began striking up conversations with anyone sitting near us.

"Don't talk to strangers," Willard whispered.

"Why?" I asked.

"Because this is New York City," he said.

"What does that matter?" I asked. "I was just being friendly."

We passed a man sitting on the sidewalk, begging, and I asked Willard if we could give him a quarter.

"No, we don't give those people money," he said. By the time we got back home, I felt sadness creeping into my heart. I loved this man, but I wasn't sure of his love for me. I was beginning to realize that my expectations for marriage were completely different from Willard's and our personalities were polar opposites.

We lived with Willard's parents for the first few months. Mrs. Price was always nice to me and I felt very comfortable with her.

Mr. and Mrs. Price went to bed early, so Willard said we should go to bed at the same time. I was young and by no means was I ready for sleep at 9 p.m. I wanted to talk or listen to the radio—and certainly make love with my new husband. However, our bedroom was right beside theirs so Willard was always cautioning me to be quiet.

Willard had a close relationship with his mom and I kind of envied that, since I had never really had that with my mother or Beulah. However, after a few months, I began feeling a wee bit jealous, and I was elated when Willard found us an apartment. It was across the alley from the Prices. Our apartment was small and on the third floor, but at least it was ours.

I had secured a job at a local sewing factory, but when I saw the stacks of material piled on my machine, I was dismayed. I didn't face any of the other workers, so for a people-person like me, it was disheartening. In spite of it, though, I made friends and worked hard at making the job fun. I must say that I absolutely hated everything about that job. It was so different from working at the restaurant where I interacted with many people during my shift.

Some of the women at work occasionally invited me to go with them to the movies and to a local bar for a drink afterwards. I told Willard that I would be going out with the girls on Friday nights and since he went to bed early it shouldn't be a problem. Willard disapproved of me going, but didn't say I couldn't go.

I enjoyed the music, the dancing and the companionship, but the atmosphere stirred up temptation in me, and I flirted unashamedly with many of the men hanging out there. However, when one guy asked me to go with him for a ride, I realized I was heading for trouble and chose not to go out with my working friends again.

To fill my Friday night gap, I chose to have Polly over. She was still unmarried and living at home and was happy to join me. We watched television together, ate cheese and crackers, talked and just basically enjoyed ourselves. Polly would stay overnight and go home in the morning.

Willard would often stop by his mom's before coming home after work. Sometimes he would even eat a slice of pie or other food and then not be hungry or interested in what I had made for dinner. I tried hard to please him, but I could not cook like his mom. His "suggestions" that I ask her for a recipe or how to do certain things hurt my feelings, but I did it anyway. I grew to love my mother-in-law and opened my heart to her wisdom.

Even though we had moved into our own place, Willard continued to retire early, leaving me alone to face long and boring evenings. I was lonely. I tried to be a good wife, but no matter how hard I tried, I felt like I could not make Willard love me. I felt betrayed.

Since divorce was completely out of the question, I began looking elsewhere to fill the void in my life. I had no trouble finding friends willing to wile away long hours with me, laughing, joking and playing cards while my handsome husband slept.

It was during those early disappointing days of my marriage that I decided to have a baby. I was determined to create the world I had never had.

I wanted my own family——babies on whom I could shower all the pent-up love in my heart. The family I envisioned would be unlike the one in which I grew up. I would not yell at my children and they would know with certainty they were loved, for I would tell them every single day. I would create a home filled with love, warmth and laughter. And there would be music! If my dream became a reality, I knew it would be completely up to me, for Willard's idea of a home and family was quite unlike mine. I couldn't wait to get pregnant.

After a year of trying, I had not conceived. I was sure something was wrong with me and I made an appointment with my doctor. After an examination and a few tests, the doctor prescribed what he called "hormone pills." In less than a year, I was pregnant. I literally sailed home to share the news with Willard.

Other than a few minor complications, my pregnancy was uneventful. The doctor started my labor when I was two weeks past my due date. After nine hours of labor, on December 23, 1958 at 8:30 p.m., Keely Ann Price, weighing 7 pounds and 4 ounces was placed in my waiting arms.

I named her after Keely Smith, a popular singer at the time, who was my idol. I had some of her records and knew most of the songs by heart. Looking back I can see that naming my daughter after a musician foreshadowed the role music would play in her life.

Keely Price was amazingly beautiful. She had

large blue eyes and wispy blond hair that framed her tiny perfect face. Carefully, I loosened her blanket, and as mothers do universally, I examined every part of her. She was everything I had dreamed of and more.

In the morning, the nurse brought a crying Keely to my bed and I attempted to nurse her, to no avail. Nothing I did seemed to comfort her and I called for the nurse to come and get her. Later, my sister came to visit and we walked together to the nursery. There were several parents and grandparents beaming through the glass at the beautiful babies. Keely was easy to spot for she was crying again and her head was arched back in an odd way. *Why? Why is she crying?* I was worried and asked the nurse why she cried so much. She simply smiled and said, "Babies cry."

I was, undoubtedly, the proudest mom that ever left Grand View Hospital in Sellersville, Pennsylvania. My perfect little girl and I returned to our home to the perfect little family I was creating. I wish I could say that's actually what happened, but perfection didn't describe the life that awaited me.

Keely had numerous problems from the start. She didn't appear strong enough to suck the milk from her bottle, and because she was hungry, she cried until

I thought my heart would surely break.

I found myself calling Dr. Thomas, Keely's pediatrician, almost on a weekly basis for one reason or another—rashes, fever, colic or crying that never seemed to stop. She was seldom content and would cry for long periods with no obvious explanation.

Willard tried to help, but he couldn't work and sit up all night with a crying baby. I was completely exhausted. *What was wrong with our daughter?*

I knew that by the time babies were four months old, they should roll over, hold up their heads and reach for objects. By four months, Keely was doing none of that. I was afraid something was wrong with my baby, although the doctor kept insisting she was fine.

When Keely was five months old, I took her for her checkup. Dr. Thomas was on vacation and a younger intern from Philadelphia was covering for him. He examined Keely, measured her head, then dangled a ring of keys above her. Keely was oblivious.

"Do you notice how your daughter doesn't reach for these keys?" he asked.

"Yes," I answered, as my heart lurched.

He pulled out a tape measure and began measuring Keely's head again. Then he looked again at her chart. "Um. . .Mrs. Price, I'm afraid Keely's head isn't growing."

I backed away, fear making me breathless, waiting for an explanation. He made no further comment, but continued examining Keely.

"Exactly what are you trying to tell me?" I asked, dreading what he would say.

"There is some concern about Keely's development," he said, looking at me with pity.

"What do you mean? Dr. Thomas has been seeing her for months and he hasn't mentioned that anything serious is wrong with Keely."

"Mrs. Price, it's easier for me to tell you this than your doctor. I am concerned that Keely either has a blood clot on the brain, a tumor or a premature closure of the soft spot." His words crushed all thoughts of my perfect family. My mind raced. I couldn't focus and my words came out in chokes.

"What do I do now?"

"Take her for x-rays," he said, smiling weakly and handing Keely to me.

I held back the tears until I was safely in the car. Crying softly and praying for the first time in years, I begged God to help me.

"Please don't let anything be wrong with her, God. Please don't!"

Arriving home, I placed Keely in the crib and stroked her back until she slept. As I stood over her, tears streaming down, I pleaded with God not to let anything be wrong with my baby. I promised Him I would stop smoking and swearing, I would go to church every Sunday, and I would be a better wife. Promises, promises—if only . . . if only Keely didn't have something wrong.

I went outside to sit on the front porch to try and gather my thoughts. I felt cheated, scared and alone. At first I didn't notice my neighbor sitting on her porch. She saw that I was upset and asked if I was okay.

"The doctor wants me to get Keely's head x-rayed," I said. "He says her head isn't growing." I could scarcely get the words past the lump in my throat.

"Claudie, you need to do whatever the doctor is telling you. I know it's upsetting, but it's best to follow his advice."

Has she noticed that something is wrong with
Keely? She must! After all, she has five kids of
her own, and she's a nurse.

That evening I broke the news to Willard and

pleaded with him to take me to the hospital for the x-rays. He insisted he couldn't afford to lose time from work, so I called my cousin, Elva. She agreed to accompany me.

After the x-rays were taken, the technician said he saw no sign of a blood clot, tumor or premature closure, but my doctor would give me the full report. What a relief!

Our apartment had been fine for the two of us, but when Keely came along, we were cramped, and lugging groceries and Keely up to the third floor had become increasingly difficult. We agreed to look for a bigger place.

We were able to secure a larger apartment and later, with the help of Willard's parents, we purchased a row home on Railroad Avenue in Souderton. It was wonderful to have more room and no steps to climb.

Keely Ann Price

Chapter Four

Disconcerting Doubts

Relief regarding Keely's x-rays didn't last long, however, for in the weeks to come, Keely did not progress normally. In my heart I knew something serious was wrong with my beautiful baby girl, but I fought against believing it.

There were numerous visits to Dr. Thomas. Keely broke out in unexplained rashes, spiked high temperatures, had stomach cramps, ear infections, bladder infections and sore throats. On three separate occasions, she was diagnosed with measles. Chronic constipation was a huge problem for her. When suppositories didn't produce a bowel movement, I was forced to manually remove the fecal matter.

Whenever Keely cried, day or night I stroked her back to comfort her until she drifted off.

Consequently, I was always exhausted.

Even though I saw Dr. Thomas almost every month, he never mentioned the x-ray report and I was afraid to ask questions, choosing to ignore the obvious.

When I shared my fear about Keely's development with family and friends, they reassured me that she was fine. I desperately wanted to believe them. It was difficult though, for other babies much younger than Keely were cooing, sitting up and playing with little toys. Keely still had to be propped up with a pillow or her head would slump down.

People asked, "How's Keely?" more and more frequently. I felt foolish, anxious and worried. In addition, I found I was pregnant again. Keely was only six months old.

The months that followed were difficult. I called Aunt Margaret more often for she was the only one who I felt understood and would take time to really listen. I know she prayed for me.

I did everything I could possibly think of to encourage Keely's development. I set our bird cage on the floor and placed Keely on her stomach to watch the bird, hoping to entice her to lift her head and crawl toward it, to no avail. Propping her here or there, teasing her with objects, standing her on legs that refused to stand— nothing worked. It was emotionally draining for Keely and me. We both broke down in tears after each session. In addition, Willard grew distant and insisted I loved Keely more than him. That only added to my stress.

I scarcely had time to prepare for a new baby, nevertheless, on April 14, 1960, my wonderful son, Kevan, was born. Keely was fifteen months old and she still could not sit up alone. I thanked God that Kevan was a normal, healthy baby.

When I went into the hospital for Kevan's birth, I had a difficult time finding someone to care for Keely. Finally, Beulah and my dad agreed to keep her, and I went to the hospital feeling at peace. After all there were several of my brothers and sisters still at home who could pitch in and help out. I knew that Daddy really loved Keely and I was sure he would tease and play with her as well. Keely loved her pop-pop.

My peace, however, was short-lived. My sister Ruby called me the day after I gave birth to tell me I had to come and get Keely.

"Why, Ruby? What's wrong?" I was so weak and my nerves were raw and on edge.

"What is it, Ruby?" I thought she would never get the words out, but finally, she managed.

"Mother is angry at Keely and is spanking her!" Ruby was crying and talking through her sobs.

"Don't you worry, Ruby. I'll take care of it."

"You won't tell Mother I called, will you Claudie? She'll really be mad."

"Of course not, Ruby. Please watch over Keely for me until someone comes for her, will you? Promise me, Ruby?

"Okay, Claudie. I promise."

Visions of what happened to my twin sister, Polly, when we were about eight years old flashed through my mind. Several of us were heading for the playground to play but since Polly was being punished for something, she wasn't allowed to come with us. However, she ran after us anyway, and in spite of Beulah screaming at her to "Get back here!" she continued running. We turned and watched Beulah run across the field and catch Polly by the arm. Polly was always small for her age and watching Beulah kick her several times as she dragged her home made me sick to my stomach.

I managed to call Willard even though my hands

shook almost uncontrollably. "Willard, I need to get home right away."

"Why, what's going on?"

"We need to get Keely and bring her home."

"You'll be coming home tomorrow. Keely will be fine," he said.

I don't remember how I got through the next twenty-four hours, but I prayed that God would protect Keely and I turned my focus to my baby boy.

Not long after I got home, Willard picked up Keely and brought her home. Because my sisters all had small children, they couldn't come and help, so I had two babies to care for as I recuperated from childbirth. Even so I felt at peace knowing Keely was safe at home with me.

Kevan was a delightful baby. He only cried when he needed something and was generally contented, peaceful and a joy to watch. God had given me another special child.

The next several months passed in a blur. I had two babies and a sullen, distant husband. Though I continued trying different tactics with Keely, by the time she was twenty months old, she could not sit alone without being propped up and she never learned to crawl. Kevan, at seven months, could sit up straight, crawl and babble a few words.

The difference between my two babies could no longer be denied in spite of what my pediatrician was saying. I had to have answers. I was tired of wondering and worrying and weary of everyone's questions. For a while, I thought maybe Keely was deaf or possibly have muscular dystrophy. I continually searched for explanations. I needed to know.

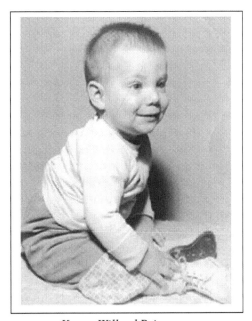

Kevan Willard Price

Kevan

Chapter Five

Shattered Dream

I made an appointment with Dr. Thomas, determined to get the truth. I would insist he do whatever necessary to find out why Keely was not developing. Again I asked Willard to go with me, but again he refused.

As I waited my turn to see the doctor, I rehearsed what I would say. But all thoughts vanished when the nurse called my name. I simply gathered up my twenty-month-old baby and laid her on the examining table, knowing I needn't worry about her falling off, for she couldn't roll over.

"What is wrong with my child?" I demanded. "I cannot wait any longer for an answer. I need to know now!"

Dr. Thomas paused, looked directly into my eyes and asked, "Do you really want to know?"

"Yes. I *need* to know."

"Claudette, I'm sorry to have to tell you, but your child is mentally retarded."

The words "mentally retarded" bounced around the room and whirled through my brain. They shattered my heart. I knew something was wrong with Keely, but I never thought she could be retarded. I began to cry and anger rose up in me.

"Why didn't you tell me? Maybe something could have been done for her sooner," I sobbed.

"What could you have done if I had told you?"

"I would have saved money and taken her to a specialist," I blurted between sobs.

"I'm so sorry, Claudette," he said quietly, "but you could not have done one thing differently."

"Why did you wait till now to tell me? You knew I was concerned."

"You were not ready to hear it sooner. You would not have believed me, but would have run from doctor to doctor. Now we can begin to work with Keely, for now you know the real issue with your daughter."

He was right. He handed me a tissue to wipe my tears and lovingly picked Keely up and placed her in my arms. "I think the first thing you should do is to join a parent group," he said.

"A parent group?"

"Yes. Other parents who have retarded children can be a source of support and encouragement for you. In addition, there are programs available for Keely where she can receive all kinds of therapy."

"Where do I find out about these programs?" I asked, feeling completely broken inside.

"Call the number on here," he said, handing me a brochure. It read "Montgomery County Association for Retarded Children (MARC)."

"They will put you in touch with a group. In the meantime, treat Keely as normally as possible. Give her experiences of all kinds. Don't keep her hidden away. Love her unconditionally, praise her for her accomplishments, and don't be ashamed of her."

"Is there a name for her kind of retardation?" I asked.

"Yes. Because Keely is lacking brain tissue, her head is small. Her diagnosis is called microcephalic syndrome. There are at least seventy-five reasons why this can occur, so don't spend time trying to discover the cause. Did you know Einstein had a small brain? Using every portion of that brain made him a genius. Keely won't be a genius, but she can certainly learn, and it's up to you to be her teacher."

There are no words to describe the depths of my despair as I made my way to the car. *Retarded. Small brain. Missing tissue. Micro...what? Microcephalia. My baby is retarded. Mentally retarded. I can't believe this has happened.*

I could scarcely see to drive home as tears poured down my face. I kept glancing at Keely lying passively beside me. *I have to tell Willard. What will he say? We have to love and accept Keely. Will he be able to? Will I?*

I Am the Disabled Child

I am the disabled child.
I am your teacher.
If you allow me, I will teach you what is really
important in life.
I will give you and teach you unconditional love.
I gift you with my innocent trust, my dependency
upon you.
I teach you about how precious this life is and about
not taking things for granted.
I teach you about forgetting your own needs and
desires and dreams.
I teach you giving.
Most of all I teach you hope and faith.
I am the disabled child.

"I Am the Disabled Child"-Author Unknown

Chapter Six

Facing the Truth

On arriving home, I placed Keely in her crib and any doubts about my ability to love this baby vanished. I stroked her back and whispered love to my sweet, helpless baby girl.

I swooped up Kevan from the playpen, held him close and thanked God that he was strong and healthy.

As the day wore on, I rehearsed a number of ways to break the news to Willard. I stood holding Keely and looking out the window as Willard arrived home from work, and all thoughts of how to tell him escaped me. I blurted out Keely's diagnosis.

Willard dropped his lunch kettle on the counter and took Keely from me.

"She's what?" asked Willard.

"Keely is mentally retarded, Willard. She has what the doctor calls microcephalia."

"That's ridiculous," he said. "Tell Mommy you will be Miss America someday," he said, tickling Keely under the chin.

"Did you hear what I just said?"

"Yes. I heard you. Do you have this in your family?"

"What are you talking about?" I said. "Just maybe it's in *your* family!" In frustration and fear, we blamed and accused one another until we were exhausted.

"I . . . I don't know what to say," Willard stammered. His eyes watered and he obviously didn't know how to respond. We were unable to comfort each other. I desperately wanted him to throw his arms around me and assure me it would be all right—that we would work through it together. Instead, he handed Keely to me, stared helplessly at us and walked away.

"Keely may be a retarded child," I shouted after him, "but she will be the best retarded child!" No answer.

I wish I felt as confident as I sounded, but I was scared and worried. *How will I make my family and friends understand and accept Keely? Would Willard stand by me? Would he love Keely? Will I be able to effectively mother both my children?* Questions whirled through my mind.

The next day I began calling some of my family. I needed to share my heartbreak. I wanted them to understand and hear them say they would be there for me. I knew they loved me, but the words I longed to hear were not spoken. Rather, I heard many well-meaning statements that tore at my heart. "There are real nice institutions for kids like Keely," was one. Another was "Don't cry, Claudie, you can place her, you know." The most hurtful, however, was, "You'll have to place her, Claudie, you have a normal baby to raise, don't forget." As if I could forget Kevan and that turning my helpless baby over to strangers to raise was no big deal.

The enormity of my situation was becoming increasingly clear. I was alone. It was *my* problem. Keely was mine—mine to train, mine to teach, mine to raise.

I had many friends and as I began sharing about Keely with them, I soon learned that they were not particularly interested in hearing about my struggles. As long as I could continue being the fun-loving Claudie, who could liven a group with her jokes and laughter, they were more than willing to listen. I learned to smile and cover up the truth of my life at an early age and I continued doing that for many years. I remember popular songs of the day, with lines such as, "Smile though your heart is breaking," and "Oh yes, I'm the Great Pretender," and felt they accurately described my life. However as the pressures of having a retarded child grew, my life took on new meaning and many friendships waned and died.

I began a reading campaign. I checked books out of the library on the subject of retardation. Every newspaper article on retarded children suddenly caught my eye. I was glued to the television when there was a program on the subject. I began noticing retarded children whenever I went out and wondered how Keely would look as she grew into womanhood. Would she remain as pretty as she is now? Would she drool, babble strange noises, rock back and forth and develop a misshapen body like some retarded children I had seen? I was learning about this new thing called, "mental retardation" and it was frightening.

Family gatherings became sources of pain for me as I listened to my sisters' talk about their children. They spoke about the "terrible twos" and I longed for my daughter to be a "terrible two." If only she *could* scamper about and get into things. I would happily trade that for the Keely sitting passively on my lap.

Some time passed before I remembered the doctor's admonition about joining a parent group. He had assured me that other parents with retarded children would be a source of support and encouragement. We could help each other. It was worth a try. I was willing to do anything that would help Keely. But would Willard? Would he go with me and participate in a parent group? I longed for his support and involvement.

"Please, Willard. Keely is *our* daughter and we both need to be involved with her care."

"Who will babysit? Besides we don't have the money to pay for a sitter."

I realized he was right. I couldn't depend on my family, although they helped when they could, and our budget was strained as it was.

"You go and I'll stay with the kids," he said. I was so disappointed, but that's exactly what we did. For the next several years, that became our pattern—I went to meetings and he stayed home with the children. I felt like it was another wall being erected between us.

"Having a handicapped child born into a family and grow into adulthood is one of the most stressful experiences a family can endure. Parental reactions to the realization that their child is exceptional usually include shock, depression, guilt, anger, sadness, and anxiety. Individuals handle each of these feelings differently and may stay in certain stages longer than others. Some parents perceive the handicapped infant as an extension of themselves and may feel shame, social rejection, ridicule or embarrassment. Parental reactions may be affected by economic status, personality traits and marital stability. In short, an initial parental response may be a form of emotional disintegration. This may evolve into a period of adjustment and later into reorganization of the family's daily life. Some parents cannot cope beyond the emotional disintegration."
Impact of a Handicapped Child on the Family, by Marcia A. Cohen; Yale-New Haven Teachers' Institute
(Curriculum Unit 82.06.08

Chapter Seven

Exploring Options

When I telephoned Montgomery County
Association for Retarded Children (MARC), I was
advised to contact Elinore Polite in Lansdale regarding
a preschool for Keely.

"A preschool? You mean that my two and a
half-year-old daughter, who is not yet able to walk,
would be permitted to attend a preschool?"

"Absolutely, Mrs. Price. Early intervention is
imperative for Keely."

I don't remember the rest of that conversation.
All I could think of was that Keely could attend a
preschool! *Would Keely be able to learn? What would
preschool cost? Could we afford it? Would Willard
agree to let her go?* Questions and more questions
raced through my mind and along with the questions,

was hope—something I had needed for a long time—hope for my Keely.

When I hung up, I wanted to shout and sing! Kevan was playing with his blocks in the middle of the living room floor. I picked him up and whirled him around in the air.

"Keely's going to school! Keely's going to school!" I chanted as Kevan giggled at my antics. Then I scooped up Keely and danced with my two babies until I was completely out of breath. All my questions vanished, for I knew I would find a way for Keely to go to school.

That evening I shared what I thought was my good news with Willard.

"Preschool! She doesn't need to go to school. You can teach her at home. Besides, we can't afford it." As I listened to Willard, I realized that he did not grasp what a tremendous responsibility it was going to be to raise a retarded daughter. Keely needed training and education and she needed it now. Willard sensed it was useless to argue with me and eventually agreed to at least look into it.

My hands trembled as I rang the doorbell of Elinore Polite's home. She was a teacher and the thought of conversing with a teacher was nerve wracking to say the least. My experience with teachers had been anything but positive. Images of my school days when teachers quizzed me about my missing homework forced their way into my mind as I waited nervously for the door to open.

Elinore Polite did little to allay my nervousness or change my impression of teachers for she appeared stern. Although her manner was authoritative, I forced myself to focus on what she had to say. I hung onto her every word and carefully noted all she had to share. It was obvious she was knowledgeable about the needs of retarded children and I grew calmer as the hour passed.

MARC sponsored several schools for retarded children in the county and Elinore was one of the teachers in the Wrens preschool. Wrens would be the best place for Keely. Before leaving, I signed papers enrolling her in the school, hoping the $35 a month would not initiate an argument between Willard and me. I knew full well that it would be a financial strain on our limited budget, for we were constantly inundated with medical bills for Keely.

When I informed Willard that I had enrolled Keely in Wrens and what the cost was, he was angry, but did not argue with me. He knew me well enough to know that when I made up my mind about something, it was useless to try and change it. I had to fight for my daughter.

I had protected and babied Keely since her birth. After talking with Elinore Polite, I realized Keely needed much more than that. She needed to develop to the full measure of her potential. At 2½ she could not walk alone, could not talk and she still wore diapers.

Kevan and Keely

As a result of some modest research efforts, we know that some fathers experience adverse reactions to the birth of a child with a disability. Fathers who are coping poorly themselves tend to find it difficult to be supportive of their spouses. When fathers experience stress and withdraw from their families, other family members (especially the mother) must take up the slack, resulting in family tensions. Furthermore, there is some evidence that fathers may cope better with a daughter than a son. . . Generally speaking, though fathers appear to adapt to their children rather well. It seems that a majority of fathers have little trouble assimilating a child with a disability into their lives, while others have learned great lessons and have grown from the experience.

Seligman, Milton & Darling, Rosalyn Benjamin, *Ordinary Families, Special Children, 2nd ed.,(pp. 156), The Guilford Press, New York, London.*

Chapter Eight

Early Intervention

As I positioned Kevan and Keely in the car for our short ride to Wrens, I was upset with Willard. He had made a last ditch effort to dissuade me from taking Keely to preschool. It hurt so much to know that he seemed unable to understand that I could not be Keely's teacher. There was so much I needed to know myself in order to help her.

Kevan could tell I was upset when his dad left for work. "Okay, Mommy. Okay, Mommy." I hadn't noticed that he had toddled over to me and was clinging to my leg. With the few words he knew, he was trying to comfort me.

"Mommy's okay, Kevan" I said, sweeping him up into my arms. "Mommy's okay."

By this time Kevan was walking, though a bit unsteady, but not so Keely. So on Keely's first day of preschool, I carried her, a diaper bag, my handbag and led Kevan along beside me across the parking lot. I was sad, curious, anxious and guilty. *Am I doing the right thing? After all, Keely is a baby. She can't walk alone, talk and for crying out loud, she still wears diapers!*

Elinore Polite greeted me at the door.

"Mrs. Price, can't your daughter walk?"

"Not really. I usually just carry her. Her legs are wobbly and weak."

"Well, let's just check out these wobbly legs," Elinore said, smiling and taking Keely from my arms. She placed Keely on her feet and together we "walked" Keely inside. I never again carried Keely into the school.

In the months following, I learned that parents have a tendency to make things too easy for their children. Children like Keely especially need to be pushed into grasping everything they can. Often that means they will cry, be uncomfortable or even get hurt.

Keely's classroom was filled with colorful toys, small tables and chairs, stuffed animals, books, puzzles and more. It was a warm and inviting room. A few children had already arrived and workers were busy involving them in activities.

Kevan spotted some toy trucks on a shelf and headed for them as fast as his little legs would carry him. Elinore showed me where to put Keely's things and then I placed Keely on a small chair. She began to cry. "It's okay, Keely. Mommy will be back soon." Elinore stepped away to take a phone call. Keely cried louder, arching her back. Another child began crying. "Oh, Keely, please don't cry," I pleaded. I started to pick her up, but Elinore was instantly by my side.

"She'll be fine, Mrs. Price. You need to go now. Keely will be fine. If there's a problem, I have your phone number," she said. I took Kevan and left, wondering if I had made a huge mistake.

I tugged on Kevan's arm hurrying in order to escape Keely's sobs still audible in the parking lot. I nodded a greeting to a lady getting into her car parked beside mine.

"Hello," she said, smiling at me. "Is this your first day at Wrens?"

"Yes. That's my daughter you hear wailing inside," I said, motioning to the building. I struggled to to control the tears threatening my eyes.

"Oh, she'll be fine. It's always that way at first. I'm Rose Icano. My daughter attends here."

"Nice to meet you. I'm Claudette Price and this is my son, Kevan."

"Hey, if you're not in a big hurry, would you like to grab a cup of coffee?"

"Sure. That would be great," I responded. I was eager for companionship at that moment.

"Hop in my car and we'll go to my place."

Rose and I spent the rest of the morning together, sharing stories about our lives and especially our retarded children. I felt for the first time, somebody understood my situation. She was living the same heartache and frustration that I was living. I was excited, encouraged and hopeful as Rose drove me back to the preschool to pick up Keely.

That day was the beginning of many mornings I would spend with parents of retarded children. Later I met Anna Gehman and Emma Stahl, also parents, who invited me to attend a monthly parent meeting where I was introduced to the group structure.

After attending my first meeting, I was hooked. I felt an immediate connection to these parents. Their pain was my pain. Their concerns were my concerns.

In addition to providing support and encouragement, the parent group was actively involved in raising money for MARC. Because there was no state funding, MARC relied on donations to provide programs for these children. In addition, parents often assisted the preschool teachers in any way they could. It was a group bound together by common concerns and I knew I had found a special group of people.

The more involved I became with the parent group, the more Willard withdrew from me. I told him I would try again to get a sitter if he would consider getting involved with me, but he declined, volunteering to stay home with Keely and Kevan instead. While that was definitely a help, I wanted him by my side, helping me make a better life for our daughter as well as for other children like her.

Kevan and Keely

Much of the information that will be helpful to you is in the hands, heads, and hearts of other parents like yourselves. For this reason, it is worthwhile to join a parent's group, which can offer you the opportunity to meet other people with children who have disabilities. . . Within each of these groups, information, emotional and practical support, and common concerns can be shared. The power of this mutual sharing to combat feelings of isolation, confusion, and stress is a consistent thread running throughout the literature written by and for parents.

Kid Source Online article: *When Your Child Has a Disability,* by Carole Brown, Samara Goodman and Lisa Kupper.

Chapter Nine

Educating Mom

Elinore Polite pulled me aside one morning as I dropped Keely off at Wrens and suggested that I might be interested in attending a monthly MARC meeting. Since joining the parent group, I had a growing desire to learn all I could about my child and was willing to go anywhere and do almost anything if it meant improving her life. Elinore gave me directions to the meeting place and I left with eager anticipation.

MARC met in Norristown about ten miles from my home. At that point in my life, I was not used to going anywhere except locally by myself. The thought of driving at night to a place I'd never been and walking alone into a meeting of strangers, especially educated people, filled me with trepidation. I begged Willard to go with me, but he flatly refused, saying we couldn't afford a sitter. I worried about what I should wear. *Should I dress up? What if they asked me questions? Would I sound stupid?* Anxious thoughts whirled through my head day after day until I almost decided not to go.

I stood in front of the mirror trying to decide if the new dress I had bought for the meeting was too long. *It is too long. I should have tried it on. It looks horrible.*

"Mommy pretty," babbled Kevan, who had been playing with a toy truck on the bedroom floor. "Mommy pretty," he repeated, studying my image in the mirror.

"Thank you, Sweetie," I said, "but Mommy doesn't feel pretty right now."

I pulled the dress over my head and tossed it on the bed. *I have nothing to wear and I'm not going. I will be completely out of place anyway.* That's when my eyes caught Keely's image in the mirror. She was lying on my bed, sound asleep. *Sweet girl, you look so . . . so normal, lying there. But you're not normal. You never will be normal. I have to help you become as normal as possible. I have to!* I realized at that moment, I had to die to my fears and do whatever I could for Keely. I would go to that meeting and I would wear my too-long dress!

Driving to Norristown, I practiced introducing myself. "Hello, I'm Claudette Price. I live in Souderton and I have a retarded daughter." *That sounds dumb.* "Hello. My name is Claudette and this is my first time to attend." *As if they didn't know that already.* A few more tries and I gave up on practicing.

On reaching the meeting room, I paused before entering, checked my hair and lipstick and walked inside. All my worrying had been pointless. I was welcomed with smiles and introductions.

I don't remember much about the message the speaker delivered that night, but I do recall her asking me to introduce myself and what brought me to the meeting. In spite of my feelings of inferiority, I was able to share my story.

I was amazed that these people, many with college degrees, were all parents of retarded children! I had been feeling as though something was surely wrong with me, having a retarded child. I felt I wasn't good enough to be here with these kinds of people. Nothing could be further from the truth. I quickly learned that people from all walks of life can have a retarded child.

There was wonderful camaraderie at the meeting. MARC was a group of caring and supportive people who shared a common goal—to improve the lives of their children and the lives of other retarded children in our county. I left that meeting feeling like I was walking on a cloud. I was excited and even more determined to devote my life to the needs of these special children.

Keely in preschool

Even when members of existing social networks and family try to be helpful, parents of handicappped children may still feel that they do not *really* understand the parents' situation. Meeting other parents of disabled children thus becomes very important to many parents after they learn about their child's disability.

Supprt groups, composed of parents of disabled children and adults serve a number of functions including:

1. alleviating loneliness and isolation
2. providing information
3. providing role models
4. providing a basis for comparison

Darling, Rosalyn Benjamin, *Initial and Continuing Adaptation to the Birth of a Disabled Child,* Allyn and Bacon, ©1991,*"Support Groups," p. 66.*

Chapter Ten

The Three R's

I had hoped that I would see dramatic changes in Keely by placing her in Wrens. For the first two weeks, each time I picked her up, I quizzed the workers. "How did she do? I hope she didn't cry for you." On Friday of the second week, Elinore Polite asked me to stay for a few minutes to talk. Thoughts of teachers telling me I was failing, zipped through my mind. I stationed Kevan with some blocks, gathered Keely's things and waited until the rest of the children were gone. *I wonder what's wrong. I hope she isn't going to tell me Keely can't be in the program.*

"Claudette, I know you are concerned about Keely's progress, so I want to explain some things to you."

"All right," I responded, feeling like I was in first grade.

"Our purpose at Wrens is to prepare Keely to enter the public school system by the time she is six years old. She will most likely attend the daycare program there and she will need certain skills to qualify." Kevan had tired of the blocks and Keely began to cry as I struggled to hang onto Elinore's every word.

"Keely needs to improve her gross motor skills; for example, standing and walking alone. She needs to be able to sit on a chair for increasingly longer periods of time. It's important for her to hold up her head and make eye contact. Those are a few extremely important goals. Potty training is another. In addition, she needs to learn how to use her hands to eat with and pick up objects. Speech is another area of concern. So you see, Claudette, Keely has a long way to go in the next few years. I want you to understand that her progress will be slow, but we do expect her to make progress. It just won't be overnight."

"What can I do to help her?" I asked, ignoring my disappointment.

"You can reinforce at home what we are doing here. We'll let you know the particular skills we are working on and you can practice them with her."

I thanked Elinore for taking the time to explain things to me. I left with a better understanding of what Wrens and I could do together to help Keely learn as much as she could in the next three years.

From then on, I watched the teachers and workers interact with Keely and tried to copy their actions at home. When they worked on sitting on a chair, I repeated the same actions. It was difficult at first watching them smack her knee lightly and say, "No!" firmly and place her back on the chair. After all she was still very much a baby. I pushed past my feelings knowing Keely would not learn anything the easy way.

In addition to Elinore Polite, there were two other teachers at Wrens whom I looked up to and considered them not only as Keely's teachers, but my friends. They were Marian Moser and Mae Drummond. All three of these ladies, whether they ever knew it or not, were almost like a mother to me and at the very least, mentors.

The workers at Wrens introduced Keely to various activities to stimulate the use of her hands that she kept clenched. She needed to learn how to use them. Rolling and kneading Playdough, stringing beads and tearing paper were three that I remember. They hoped that noisy paper tearing would help lengthen Keely's attention span as well. The day she finally tore paper was a huge event. Little did I know how her new skill would become a test of my patience. Her delight in tearing paper in the years following meant no paper in our house was safe. I had to rescue bills, newspapers and magazines before she could scramble over and tear them to shreds. When Kevan started school, his homework and artwork had to be kept out of her reach or she would tear them to her heart's content.

Keely learned lip control by blowing bubbles into a glass of water. Every single activity was a difficult challenge. Nothing came easy for Keely, for her teachers or for me.

Keely eventually learned how to pick up her food and eat with her hands. However, if I didn't cut her sandwiches into small pieces, she would grab a handful and stuff it all in her mouth at once. She never learned to really *chew* her food, rather, almost swallowing it whole. This created a great deal of stomach problems that increased as she grew older.

Keely could not talk, make gestures or express herself other than crying or laughing. Thus, potty training was one of the most difficult tasks to master. For years I put her on the potty and encouraged her to go. I demonstrated straining over and over. On the rare occasions when she went, I danced around, praised her as she giggled with delight. In the next half hour, she would be wet. The workers at Wrens consistently worked with her as well, but it wasn't until she was five that I can say she was potty trained. Even then, she had frequent accidents.

In preschool, Keely never learned to string beads, put puzzle pieces together or play games with the other children. She was not successful in learning to march or skip, but she did learn to jump.

One thing that I had discovered early on with Keely was her response to music. Even as young as two, I would catch her rocking with the beat. When she was five, I caught her humming a tune and her pitch was perfect!

Two speech therapists taught me how to develop Keely's speech at home. I spent hours with her, day after day, trying to get her to say "ball." Over and over I tossed her the ball, repeating "ball" each time. It was difficult and frustrating for both of us, and Keely usually ended up crying and refusing to cooperate. The therapists agreed that my efforts at home probably wouldn't work, although Keely did eventually learn to say "ball." They felt that Keely had a condition called expressive aphasia that allows her to understand many things, but unable to release a verbal response.

Every tiny step forward that Keely made required time, energy, patience and consistency for me and the workers at Wrens. For Keely it meant tears, temper tantrums, painful falls, scrapes, and occasional stitches.

While reviewing Keely's progress one day with her teacher, I was introduced to the concept of Repetition, Relaxation and Routine—the three R's. All three were necessary to aid Keely's progress. For me, these were a challenge, for I was always in a hurry. I had to constantly remind myself that Keely needed me to be patient, repeat an action over and over and stay as relaxed as possible. I could not rush her and if I tried, it inevitably led to a melt down either by her or me.

When the teacher quizzed me about Keely's bedtime routine, I had to confess that I refused to allow Keely to cry in her crib because I did not want her to wake up Kevan.

"Mrs. Price, Keely needs to have you establish a bedtime routine. Otherwise, she will never learn to go to sleep on her own without you rocking her. Please put her in her crib and allow her to learn to go to sleep without being rocked. She will cry, and it won't be easy, but you need to do this for her." I remember being close to tears, thinking that I was failing as a mother.

I tried to put into practice everything the teachers suggested I do with Keely, but I was not always successful.

Willard worked night shift during this time so almost all of Keely's home training fell on me for Willard had to sleep during the day. Even when he was available, he insisted that I could do a better job training Keely than he could. In addition, I believe he didn't agree with the training methods I had learned from the Wren's teachers. It was difficult for him to understand that Keely needed correction when she did something wrong and that meant a smack on her bottom and a firm scolding.

Since I had become more active, I spent more evenings away from home and our phone rang constantly. This did not set well with Willard either.

"You should spend more time at home instead of running all over the place," he would say.

So to try and keep peace, I took great pains in trying to make Willard happy in other ways, for I still had hopes that he and I could have a loving, supportive marriage, working harmoniously for the good of our children. I stayed up late every night, drinking coffee in order to keep awake. In order for Willard to have desserts with his dinner, it was not unusual for me to bake a pie or cake at midnight. I did much of my cleaning, washing and ironing after he and the children had gone to bed. I sincerely wanted to please Willard, to have him admire and respect me, but no matter how hard I tried, he never seemed really happy with me. In addition to resenting my involvement with anyone or anything outside our home, I felt he resented the time I devoted to our children. I couldn't do anything right.

Keely at Camp

Preschool Education

For the child with a disability, formal education may begin shortly after birth. With the proliferation of early intervention programs in recent years, many children have begun receiving services soon after or even before they are diagnosed. These programs may be either home based or center based, although programs of both kinds typically involve parents as teachers for their own children. Some programs include specialists, such as physical or speech therapists, in addition to specially trained teachers.

Today, Public Law 99-457 and other funding sources have made preschool education more available, and physicians and other professionals are better informed about the existence of local programs.

Seligman, Milton & Darling, Rosalyn Benjamin, *Ordinary Families, Special Children, 2nd ed., (pp. 156), The Guilford Press, New York, London.*

Chapter Eleven

Meeting the Life-Giver

Carolyn Bergey was a friend I met during the early years of my marriage. She and I connected immediately. Her infectious laugh and warm personality made her a delight to be around. Many mornings after dropping Keely off at preschool, I would drop by Carolyn's for coffee and a cigarette. She always had my ashtray ready and the coffee hot.

On one of these drop-in visits to Carolyn's, I breezed in, tossed my jacket on a chair and dug in my purse for my cigarettes and lighter.

"What's new, Carolyn?" I asked, popping a cigarette in my mouth, and dropping onto a chair.

"Actually, there is something very new," she said, beaming at me. She had a Bible open in front of her. "I got saved last night."

"You got what?" I asked.

"I trusted Jesus as my Savior."

"You're not going to be one of those fanatics, are you, Carolyn?" I asked. She laughed.

Even though Aunt Margaret had continued to encourage me to go to church, I found it easier to stay home on Sundays rather than go through the hassle of getting the children ready. Consequently, I didn't attend often, but I did believe in Jesus and sometimes I prayed.

Carolyn started to read some verses to me and talking to me about getting saved. I listened, but couldn't concentrate. Sadness crept in. What was happening to my friend? She was different and I didn't like what I was seeing or hearing. I had already begun missing the bubbly Carolyn. I stubbed out my cigarette and made an excuse to get out of there. It seemed that my whole life had been filled with pain, disappointment and loss. Now I felt like I was losing again.

Nothing could be further from the truth, however. I did not lose Carolyn as my friend. She continued supporting me in my work with retarded children and our friendship grew in spite of our differences. She never missed an opportunity, though, to tell me that I needed to have a personal relationship with Jesus.

"You need to get saved, Claudie. Otherwise, you'll end up in Hell." That was her ominous message and I thought she was fanatical.

On April 11, 1965, Carolyn telephoned me to invite me to go to a talk about the salvation needs of the handicapped. Of course, that caught my attention—anything to help Keely.

"When and where?" I asked.

"It's at my church—Sunday afternoon at four." I groaned. I had heard that Carolyn's church was one of those legalistic churches.

"I don't know, Carolyn . . . "

"Give it some thought. It will be interesting and informative, I'm sure," she said.

"Promise me I won't have to say anything or be pressured into doing anything?"

She laughed again. "Claudie, what do you mean by 'pressured'?"

"You know what I mean."

"Okay. I promise."

I agreed to go and Carolyn offered to pick me up, probably because she thought I might back out. "Remember what you promised," I whispered to her.

She nodded and smiled.

The "talk" lasted about forty-five minutes and although it was interesting, I didn't feel it was applicable to Keely. I was anxious to be on my way and stood to leave.

"We can't leave now, Claudie. Church is just beginning to start."

"Church?" I gasped. "I didn't agree to a church service," Carolyn.

"Claudie, it's only one hour," Carolyn pleaded.

"Okay, okay," I said giving her a little frustrated nudge and sat back down.

People began filling the pews as a pianist pounded out a rousing rendition of "Victory in Jesus." The pastor and song leader took their places. I checked my watch and searched in my purse for a piece of gum. "Is it all right if I chew gum?" I whispered. Carolyn shook her head and chuckled.

"Of course," she said. "This isn't prison." I smothered a laugh.

After some familiar hymns, the pastor opened his Bible and announced he would be reading from the book of Romans. Carolyn paged in her Bible to find the passage, and then held it for me to read along.

During the next thirty minutes, my life was completely changed. The pastor preached a powerful sermon that clearly impressed me with my need for a Savior. Of course, I knew about Jesus since I was a young girl. I went to vacation Bible school several summers and also to Sunday school, but I could not understand why God let my mommy die or why my stepmother was so mean if He loved me. I certainly didn't know that I needed to accept Jesus as my own personal Savior.

The moment he stopped speaking, everyone stood and the pianist began playing a closing hymn. The pastor asked that if anyone would like to receive Jesus as Savior, they should come forward. I didn't hesitate. Tears streamed down my face as I took the pastor's hand. He led me to a lady who took me to a private room and shared God's plan of salvation with me. I prayed and asked God to forgive my sins and come into my heart and save me. A sense of God's presence filled me at that moment. I was ecstatic! I was a child of God! I couldn't wait to tell Carolyn.

"I'm so happy for you, Claudie," choked Carolyn. She had been crying.

"How can I ever thank you, my friend? My life

is changed. I can feel it. I'm anxious to go home and share the news with Willard."

I knew that Jesus was my answer for all the fear, frustration and emptiness of my life. I knew I could now handle anything that life handed me. Later I learned that was in the Bible!

Willard had already gone to bed by the time I arrived home. I crept up the stairs, hoping I wouldn't wake the children, and slipped into bed beside him.

"Willard, something amazing happened to me tonight at Carolyn's church."

"What happened?" he murmured, sleepily.

"I got saved. I went forward at Carolyn's church, and I prayed to receive Jesus as my Savior."

"You what!" he said, now clearly awake.

"Ssh! You'll wake up the kids."

"I got saved. That's what. I'm a new person."

"Who saw you?" he gasped.

"What do you mean by that? Everybody there saw me." By then I didn't care if the kids *did* wake up.

"I mean anybody we know—our friends and neighbors. Gee whiz, Claudie, they're a bunch of fanatics at that church." With an exasperated sigh, he turned over and went back to sleep.

I had hoped that Willard would be happy for me or at least try and understand, but he did neither. Hurt and disappointed, I slid out of bed and went downstairs.

I rummaged through the bookcase and found the Bible Aunt Margaret had given me. I read until the wee hours of the morning, but even then I was too excited to sleep. I knew I had much to learn about this new life of mine, and it would be found in these precious pages.

God had used Keely, my life-changer to lead me to Jesus, my Life-giver. I bowed in prayer and thanked the Lord for giving my life meaning, purpose, clarity and most of all hope.

Carolyn Bergey

Even Jesus Christ experienced stress. In fact, His state of psychological stress was so severe that it has since been written about in medical journals: Hematohidrosis is a condition in which the blood vessels around sweat glands dilate to the point of rupture, whereupon the blood flows into the sweat glands – coming out as droplets of blood mixed with sweat.

This is a physical phenomenon not frequently experienced, even in the most stressful circumstances. Yet, Jesus found Himself sweating blood on the evening before His crucifixion.

During this period of time, Jesus demonstrated for every Christian how God equips a saint to think about, walk through, and succeed when under necessary STRESS:

S – Scared to death of the
T – Time just ahead, yet
R – Resolving to
E – Exude grace while being willing to
S – Sacrifice our very life, if need be, to
S – Succeed in God's goals for us.

February 16, 2009 by Dana Baily,
http://livingstonesministries.wordpress.com/2009/02/1
6/jesus-method-for-dealing-with-stress/

Chapter Twelve

Willing to Serve

A day or two following my salvation experience, two men from Carolyn's church knocked on our front door. "Come in," I said, painfully aware that Kevan and Keely had scattered toys everywhere and the radio was blaring.

"Mrs. Price, we want to let you know how happy we are that you have trusted Christ as your personal Savior."

"I'm so thankful that Carolyn invited me to go with her to church. I realize I have so much to learn and I can't wait to get started," I said.

"Here's a brochure of the various classes we offer," one of the men said. "It's a good idea to attend Sunday School every Sunday. There are classes for your children as well."

The visit was short because they could see I was busy and had my hands full. I thanked them and they prayed with me over the squeals of Keely.

I studied the brochure they left. It was true. They had a class for everyone. There was just something about the men who stopped by—I couldn't put my finger on it. My heart was absolutely overflowing with joy! Yet, these men didn't seem to be joyful. Weren't they believers? What was it about their manner that troubled me? Where was their happiness— their warmth?

I began praying for wisdom to know what church I should become a part of. I wanted to do the right thing. By the following Sunday, I sensed God leading me to return to the church Willard and I had been occasionally attending.

Everything was new! It was as though blinders had been removed from me. Faith had opened my heart and my eyes! I sang the hymns for the first time understanding the truth behind the words. Each part of the service was meaningful and created in me a thirst to know more about this new faith walk.

A few weeks went by and I "itched" to *do* something at church. I was no longer content to sit and listen. I had to get involved. I wanted to share my new faith. So after dropping Keely and Kevan at preschool one day, I drove over to church and strolled into the secretary's office. She welcomed me with a smile.

"Good morning, Claudette. Can I do something for you?"

"I really hope so. I want to teach. Is there a class that needs a teacher? I think I can do this and I'm anxious to tell children about Jesus." I knew I was talking fast and a bit nervous, but I couldn't help it. I was about to burst with the excitement of my new faith.

"Why, Claudette, have you had an *experience?*" she asked.

"Oh yes!" I exclaimed. "I am a new Christian."

"That's wonderful, Claudette."

"I've been wondering about something," I asked. "Why don't we have an altar call here—a time when people are invited to come and find out how to become a Christian?" She really had no answer for me other than to say her husband didn't believe in doing things that way. I wondered then exactly how people did get saved here.

It didn't take long for me to be invited to co-teach a Sunday School class of 4- and 5-year-old children. I delved into my new position with great enthusiasm. In my already too-busy days, I managed to carve out time to plan lessons that kept the attention of wiggly little kids, fun activities that they delighted in and most of all, sharing about the One who loved them —Jesus.

The women's mission group director approached me in the hall one Sunday morning. I had Keely by one hand and Kevan by the other and lugging a shoulder bag full of Sunday School supplies.

"Claudette, many of us realize what a wonderful job you're doing with the children here at church. We know it can't be easy since you have . . ."

"You mean since I have a retarded child?" I smiled at her.

"Yes—a retarded child. That's why I want to ask you a favor."

"Okay," I said. What is it?" Keely struggled to break free of my grip and my bag threatened to drop and spill all over the floor.

"Would you consider coming and giving a talk at our group meeting next month?"

"Me? About what?" I asked.

"About Keely."

"What do you mean, 'about Keely?'" I asked.

"Well, what it is like to have a . . ."

"Retarded child." Again I finished her sentence. I noticed many people were afraid to use the word "retarded" thinking it somehow insulted me. The truth is that Keely is retarded and I wanted people to understand that retardation is not a curse or something to be ashamed of.

I agreed to speak and attended the meeting with great trepidation. A few minutes into the talk, I began to relax and words poured out of me. The faces of the ladies revealed their interest and afterwards, expressed their enthusiastic support.

From that meeting forward, I received invitations to speak at various community organizations and PTA meetings. My life swirled with commitments and I loved every minute of it.

When Wrens closed for the summer, I realized there was a need for a summer program for the children. I approached the staff at church and asked for permission to use the church facilities to begin a summer camp for them. They agreed and I enlisted volunteers to assist. In all, I ran the camp for four years and had approximately twenty children ranging in age from 3 to10.

While driving by the YMCA one day, I got the idea for a Saturday program for retarded children at the Y. When I approached them with the idea, they agreed and again I enlisted volunteers. We held a two-hour program on Saturday mornings for approximately three years.

Every time I spoke at a meeting, I explained the need for funding and the issues involved in having a retarded child. For years these children had been kept hidden away from society and thus there was a tremendous need for information and awareness.

I continued attending the monthly meetings at MARC and was elected as second vice president. That meant I had to attend board meetings to discuss various issues and fund-raising functions. Each time I went to a meeting I was a bundle of nerves. Even though I had achieved a degree of success speaking in front of people, still I felt inferior to those on the board. Until I became a Christian, I usually chugged a shot of alcohol in the car before entering the meeting. I felt it helped me think clearly and cope with my feelings.

As the months slipped away, I became completely immersed in causes for the retarded.

Because there was no state funding for retarded children, any programs or events for them had to be funded through the community. Hence, I was always involved in some kind of fund-raising event and our phone rang constantly.

In spite of my busyness, I managed to make our home a happy place for Kevan and Keely. Kevan made friends easily and he often had several children in to play. I allowed them to have fun, not worrying about how messy things were. Toys were usually scattered everywhere. I helped them make a tent in the yard, bought a little pool for them, provided art supplies and encouraged them to draw and paint. They loved to play dress up and pretend. And always, there was music!

Becoming a Christian changed the way I approached disciplining Kevan. It became routine for me to pull him aside when he had done something wrong and lovingly explain what the Bible had to say about that behavior. Then I would hold his little hand and pray a short prayer with him.

Due to Keely's overwhelming needs, it was difficult to divide my time between her and Kevan. I did my best, but as the years went by, I found that Kevan had a way of getting attention for himself. In many photographs, I was so focused on making Keely look "normal" that I didn't notice that Kevan had his eyes crossed or was making a funny face.

Sadly, the more active I became, the more distant Willard became. I knocked myself out to please him to avoid his sullen behavior. I mowed the grass, shoveled snow, cooked a delicious dinner every night and had the toys all picked up so he wouldn't yell at Kevan when he came home. Nothing worked. He was never a happy man. I still loved him. I longed for him to come in the door and ask me about my day, draw me into his arms and tell me he loved me, and that he was proud of me. It never happened. He made me feel like I failed as a wife and mother. When Kevan fell and broke his collar bone, Willard implied it might not have happened if I had been home instead of running here and there. One thing for sure, I had been running here and there. It had become my life, but not one I had planned or wanted.

Chapter Thirteen

Surgery

By the time Keely was four years old, she had suffered through dozens of colds, sore throats and ear infections. Because she had so much drainage, I kept a small suction bulb nearby so I could clear her nasal passages. After a particularly lengthy bout of fever and sore throat, Dr. Thomas recommended that Keely have her tonsils and adenoids removed. He scheduled the surgery for the following week.

Most mornings were hectic at our home, but the day of Keely's surgery was even more so. I fixed breakfast for Kevan and Willard, dressed myself and tried not to focus on Keely's whining. She was hungry and very cranky. I couldn't give her anything to eat, though, because of the surgery. By 8 o'clock I finally had the children in the car and ready to go.

I tried to ignore Keely's whimpers as I drove to the hospital. A friend volunteered to watch Kevan and I dropped him off on the way.

The nurses at Grand View Hospital were wonderful with Keely. They teased her and in only a few minutes had her laughing as they prepared her for the operating room. When they wheeled her away, I began praying that there would be no complications and that God would protect my little girl.

In about two hours, the operation was over. I fully expected to see Keely either asleep or at least groggy from the anesthesia, but Keely was wide awake! The doctor shared the results of the surgery with me.

"Mrs. Price, Keely did not respond to the anesthesia as we expected. We could never get her completely sedated, but the operation went well."

"You mean Keely was awake during the whole thing?" I asked, incredulously.

"Not completely awake, nor completely under. However, she didn't cry or act as though she was in pain. Apparently, Keely does not possess a normal awareness of pain. We had to exercise caution because Keely's brain is small and too much anesthesia could cause greater damage," he continued. "She'll be fine in a few days. Give her soft foods to eat and plenty of fluids to drink. Oh, one more thing, Keely's adenoids were enlarged. They were the size of an 8-year-old child's. It's good we got them out."

I thanked the surgeon and thanked God for answering my prayer. Another ordeal was over. Keely spent one night in the hospital and, of course, I stayed with her.

Keely recuperated nicely and in a day or two was eating normally. She even grabbed a pretzel and downed it the day after the surgery before I could stop her. So I think the doctor was correct in saying her pain response is not typical. She does feel pain, but apparently she is able to tolerate it to a greater degree than most people.

Thankfully, Willard was willing to help me. If she needed watching, feeding, rocking—whatever—most of the time, I could count on him. In many ways he was overprotective of her, especially if she wasn't feeling well.

Life-long considerations for a child with microcephaly:
There is no treatment for microcephaly that will return the baby's head to a normal size or shape. Since microcephaly is a life-long condition that is not correctable, management includes focusing on preventing or minimizing deformities and maximizing the child's capabilities at home and in the community. Positive reinforcement will encourage the child to strengthen his/her self-esteem and promote as much independence as possible. The full extent of the problem is usually not completely understood immediately after birth, but may be revealed as the child grows and develops.

Children born with microcephaly require frequent examinations and diagnostic testing by their physician to monitor the development of the head as the child grows. The medical team works hard with the child's family to provide education and guidance to improve the health and well being of the child.
University of Virginia Health System;
http://www.healthsystem.virginia.edu/uvahealth/peds_neuro/microcep.cfm

Chapter Fourteen

Music, Music, Music

There was one thing I remember about my step-mother that I treasure, and that was her love of music. She played country music most of the time and also loved listening to the polka hour on the radio. There was almost always some kind of music playing in our home. Consequently, I learned to love music and knew almost every popular song of the day.

On Saturday nights, Daddy and Beulah often went out dancing, making sure all of us kids were tucked in bed before they left. One night, they had no sooner cleared the driveway than we popped out of bed. Did we ever have fun! We sang, jitterbugged, played, laughed and had a great time—one of our few chances to be children. Suddenly, Beulah appeared in the front door, arriving to lights burning and kids bouncing around like Mexican jumping beans.

"What-is-going-on-here!" Beulah screamed.

Instantly, the light went out and the five of us dove for our beds, chilled by her threatening voice.

As I got older and married, my love of music continued. Whenever Judy Garland had a special television performance, I stayed glued to the screen; Arthur Godfrey with his ukulele captured my heart. I didn't have time to watch much television, but when a musical special came on, I would ask Willard if we could watch it. Even though he did not share my love of music, he was always considerate and sacrificed his programs. Keely and Kevan would sit on my lap and soak up whatever I watched.

Because I loved music so much, whenever possible, I cranked up the stereo, radio or television and sang along. Both Kevan and Keely were delighted when I swept up first one and then the other, and waltzed around the room singing at the top of my lungs.

When Keely was about six-years-old, I caught her sitting in front of the television, watching The Lawrence Welk show. The musician was singing a rendition of "Tea for Two," and Keely was singing along! She wasn't clearly enunciating the words, but it was obvious she knew the song, had the tune down perfectly and was trying to vocalize.

I was so excited and scrambled to find my tape recorder and plug it in, but by the time I did that, the song had ended. However, when the next performer began singing, I pressed "play" and caught her singing, "Catch a Falling Star!"

When I took the tape to share with Keely's teachers, they were just as excited as I. "Keely, that's wonderful! Listen to Keely sing! Wow!" They clapped and praised her over and over. They understood what I knew. My daughter had a special gift, and I wanted the world to know that my little girl could sing!

Although I played the tape for many friends and family, their level of enthusiasm about Keely's attempts to communicate was disappointing. I suppose only a mother who had never heard her child say, "Mommy, I love you," or "Mommy, I don't feel good," could appreciate any glimmer of hope her child may demonstrate.

Keely and Mommy

Chapter Fifteen

Hope for the Helpless

Little by little, programs for retarded children were added to public education as communities became aware of their needs. In previous years, the responsibility for training and teaching was completely up to the parents. If their children were severely retarded, some families placed them in institutions, but most kept their children at home and coped the best way they knew how. When the county and the state began providing services, funding for teachers and programs, these parents at last received badly needed help and support.

Parents who have retarded children at home face a daily grind of bathing, feeding, dressing, toileting and training a child, who may have grown almost as tall as the parents! In spite of increased funding, the financial burden they face is huge. Because most retarded children have a variety of health problems, there are countless trips to the doctor and hospital for medicine and treatment. Also, the emotional strain a family with a retarded child faces often drives a wedge between husband and wife and many times it leads to divorce.

Occasionally, Dr. Thomas would refer me to a home where a retarded child had been born to give hope and encouragement to the parents by sharing my story. I met many parents during the years who needed a shoulder to cry on and a thread of hope to cling to. In the process, I witnessed all kinds of sights.

In one home, I visited the parents kept their son in a room with no furniture. They had cut the door in half so that he could not get out, but they could still keep sight of him. He had nothing at all to play with and nothing to do but jump and roll on the floor. His diaper was soaked and the room reeked of urine.

I recall another home where a weary mother was watching television with her retarded daughter. She was rubbing her daughter's back and talking softly to her. Her love was obvious and was reflected in her daughter's sweet, trusting smile.

Several parents I met seemed to be ashamed of

their child, and obviously needed help.

My overall impression, though, was that most of these parents loved their children, wanted the best for them, but were totally bewildered by the demanding responsibility of their care. I encouraged each of them to take advantage of the programs and services that had become available for their children.

I met some special parents through MARC. One of these was Ann Bernotes and her son, Greg, who was about Keely's age. Greg was very active and Ann had a difficult time keeping up with him. She became a good friend and was always willing to help with our fund-raising campaigns in any way she could.

Mary Fretz was another parent I met at MARC. She, too, became a close friend as we enjoyed coffee and discussed ways to help our children.

The Shumakers, Davis's, Jantons, Gehmans, Yerks, Stahals and Brazicks were some of the other parents who became friends and co-workers as well. Even though our children had different types of retardation, we all suffered similarly. Our dreams for our children had been crushed, yet we were committed to work on their behalf because unconditional love triumphed.

Blessings in Disguise are Difficult to Recognize

God sends his "little angels" in many forms and guises,
They come as lovely miracles that God alone devises.

For he does nothing without purpose, everything's a perfect plan
To fulfill in bounteous measure all he ever promised man.

For every "little angel" with a body bent and broken,
Or a little mind retarded, or little words unspoken,

Is just God's way of trying to reach and touch the hand,
Of all who do not know him and cannot understand.

That often through an angel whose wings will never fly,
The Lord is pointing out the way to his eternal sky.

Where there will be no handicaps of body, soul or mind,
And where all limitations will be dropped and left behind.

So accept these "little angels" as gifts from God above,
And thank him for his lesson in faith and hope and love.
Author Unknown

Chapter Sixteen

Stepping Stones

By the time Keely reached age six, she was eligible for the public school program. Wrens had been a wonderful experience for her, and she had progressed in many ways. I, too, had learned what she was capable of and how to supplement and reinforce her training when she was at home.

I enrolled Keely in the Souderton School District's Daycare Program. The program was originally held in the Chestnut Street School under the direction of Miss Betsy Moyer. Miss Moyer was a wonderful teacher who was immediately drawn to Keely. She took considerable interest in Keely, even coming to the house to see her on several occasions. However, when the new E. Merton Crouthamel building was built, the Daycare Program was transferred there, and Mrs. Lola Huntsinger became Keely's new teacher.

Lola, too, was a wonderful woman who was an inspiration to me in so many ways. She studied special education later in life and dedicated herself to special education students. She phoned me frequently encouraging me and offering valuable information regarding Keely's progress at school. I valued her wisdom and did my best to implement her advice.

Special Olympics was dear to her heart and I will never forget watching Keely for the first time, running (with help), laughing and doing her best to cross the finish line.

Willard and I had paid for Keely's preschool for almost four years, but that changed when she entered public school. It was a huge relief for us financially when we no longer had that expense.

Keely was quite small for her age when she entered the Souderton Daycare Program, and she still needed some support when walking. Because she was sweet-natured, cute and petite, the workers were immediately drawn to her. All of the children in her daycare class were bigger than Keely, and several were aggressive toward others. The workers took great care to protect her since she had no comprehension of self-protection; nevertheless, it was not unusual to find unexplained bruises on her.

The teachers devised and implemented programs for each child. For Keely, her daily routine included the things she had worked on in preschool plus additional skills. She had not mastered eating with utensils. She could manage a spoon somewhat, but when workers weren't looking, she would likely drop it and shove the food into her mouth with her hands. Teaching her to chew before swallowing proved to be a huge challenge. She still gummed her food and swallowed much of it whole.

Walking, running, skipping and hopping were all included in her program. She did learn to walk without assistance, but we always had to be sure she didn't trip and fall. She never learned to skip or hop, but could run with encouragement. She ran in the Special Olympics and enjoyed the laughter and excitement. Workers ran beside and behind her in the event she took a tumble. Unless Keely wasn't feeling well, she always tried hard to cooperate in whatever activity she was working on.

Keely's fine motor skills were extremely

compromised. However, given the level of her retardation, she never learned to write her name, even though she was encouraged to do that every day at school. If she was given a crayon and paper, she might make a few scribbles, then either put the crayon in her mouth or sit and watch others.

Teaching Keely to dress herself was part of her daily routine, too. In spite of the years spent encouraging her to put on her shirt, shoes and socks, she made little or no progress. She could put one arm in her jacket with prompting, but couldn't manage the other arm. Everything the teachers worked on with her at daycare, I reinforced at home.

One afternoon, while picking up Keely from school, her teacher asked to speak to me. Of course, the old apprehension swept over me.

"Claudette, I know you sing with Keely at home, but do you converse with her as well?"

I was dumbfounded. I hadn't really thought about talking *with* Keely. I was still trying to teach her words, but not in the context of conversation. From then on, I began talking with her as though she could understand everything I was saying. Surprisingly, I felt that she was able, at times, to grasp the gist of my words. I remember the first time I asked her to shut the door for me.

"Keely, shut the door for Mommy, okay?" She promptly got up and closed the door. I was astounded, and I knew then that there was comprehension on some level in Keely's brain.

She learned to copy my mannerisms and the tone of my voice. For example, if I asked, "Keely, did you have fun at school today?" She might respond, by sitting at the table and crossing her legs as though she was invited to share a cup of coffee with me.

"Uh-huh," she would say, smiling. Then I might just ask her if she saw a big pink elephant and she would respond the same way.

By the time she was twelve-years-old, she had learned 10-15 words. She could say, pool, Bo Bo (our dog), baby, truck, ball, mommy, good and a few more.

Keely loved Kevan and the minute she saw him, her eyes would light up and she would start giggling. My goal was to teach him to be patient and affectionate with his sister, as well as to protect her and be proud of her. He was a wonderful little brother and Keely absolutely adored him.

One afternoon, Kevan came home from school

and was in an unusually solemn mood. He had just begun first grade. I hoisted him up to the kitchen counter, sure something was wrong.

"Did something happen today, Kevan?" His lower lip quivered and tears poured down his cheeks.

"Everybody's making fun of me," he sobbed.

"What do you mean, Kevan? Who's making fun of you?"

"They said I was retarded. They called me retarded," he sniffled. I hugged him and dried his tears.

"Kevan, the kids in your class don't know you have a retarded sister. What they said had nothing to do with you and Keely. They were just being mean. Sometimes kids say things like that. You'll just have to forget it." That was all it took for him to hop down and head outside to play.

When I met his teacher, she told me how proud Kevan was of his sister and also his mom. "Sometimes Kevan gets on his little soapbox and fills us in on his big sister."

Keely's adoration of her brother transferred to other boys in her room, often reaching out to kiss them. (Yes, she learned the art of a smooch!) She seemed drawn to males much more so than females. She often reached out her arms to them even if she didn't know them. This was a concern for me and for her teachers so we began working on boundaries with her, but were never sure she understood.

Kevan and Keely

While Willard was gentle with Keely, he was different with his son. Much of the time he was stern with Kevan, scolding him for one reason or another, correcting him or expecting too much of him.

Because Willard worked the night shift and had to sleep during the day, he was seldom around to play with Kevan.

"Willard, he's your little boy. Please find time to play with him," I begged. At times, he tried, but it usually ended with Willard pointing out something Kevan had done wrong.

Every year the school administered a test to determine Keely's progress. Her IQ would hover around 25 and her mental age at 12 months.

Keely's health continued to be a big challenge. After repeated bladder infections, the doctor ordered x-rays and a CAT scan. The tests revealed she had three kidneys and only two ureters. The third kidney was non-functioning and the doctor felt that was the cause of the infections, but nothing could be done about it. Therefore, she was administered antibiotics frequently.

As time passed, Keely came down with a variety of health issues. Every single day presented its challenges when it came to Keely's health. If something was going around at school, I could pretty well count on Keely catching whatever it was. By this time, I felt as though the doctor's office was my second home.

Keely began having short staring episodes followed by jerking motions. Of course, since this was something new, the first time it happened it frightened me. Shortly thereafter, she was diagnosed with petit mal seizure disorder.

When Keely entered the public school system,

much of my involvement with fund-raising ceased; however, I continued reaching out to parents who had retarded children. Their responsibilities were great and they always needed encouragement. Often it was a two-way street because I benefited from their caring words.

Chapter Seventeen

Why Lord?

I always regretted that I dropped out of school and didn't graduate with my class. Sharing my feelings with a friend over coffee one day, she advised me to go for my GED. I knew others who had done that, but I never thought I could actually do it myself. I guess I needed her nudge for I could hardly wait until she was gone, so I could call the school district office to find out what I had to do to enroll in a class. The guidance counselor told me the class would be starting soon and would meet three times a week.

When I walked into the classroom that first night, I was nervous and anxious. However, those feelings dissipated, and I found myself enjoying the lessons and the other students.

One afternoon, I was reviewing the math homework, just three weeks into the class, when Kevan and Keely's seven-year-old cousin, Jay, came over to play. The boys pleaded with me to allow them to go to the store to buy candy. To get to the store they had to cross a busy street and for that reason, I was reluctant to give them permission.

"Please, Mom, we'll look both ways before crossing," begged Kevan.

"I'm allowed to cross the street," Aunt Claudie," said Jay.

In spite of my feelings of apprehension, I agreed to let them go. As soon as they ran out the door, I began praying for them. Within minutes, Jay came tearing in the back door.

"Aunt Claudie! A woman hit Kevan!" I thought he meant that Kevan had been rude to some woman and she had smacked him.

"Where is he, Jay? Why didn't Kevan come home with you?"

"N-no," said Jay, who had begun to sob. My heart rattled in my chest as blood rushed to my head.

"Jay! Where is Kevan?"

"A woman hit him with her car." His words came in chokes.

"Jay, run upstairs and wake up your Uncle Willard. Tell him he needs to watch Keely while I go get Kevan."

I dashed out the back door and down the alley and realized my breath was coming in gasps as I saw the cars backed up on the street and heard the wail of a nearby ambulance.

"He's my son!" I said, pushing through the crowd that had already gathered. I dropped down beside him and saw that his femur bone was protruding through his pants, but fortunately he was conscious.

"You're going to be all right, Kevan. The ambulance is on its way," I said stroking his head and checking him for other injuries.

"Mom, I tore my pants."

Kevan's pants were the least of my worries at that moment, but it concerned him, even more than his broken leg. I suppose it was because I often reminded him to be careful with his pants. It seemed he was always coming in with a rip or scuffed knees in them. He could destroy a good pair in a day.

"It doesn't matter about the pants, Kevan. It's okay," I said.

The woman who hit Kevan felt terrible about

the accident.

"He came out of nowhere," she said. "I slammed on my brakes, but I just couldn't stop in time." Kevan propped up his head and looked at her.

"You sure have good brakes, lady," he said. She managed a slight smile and said she hoped he wasn't hurt too badly.

The EMT's loaded Kevan into the ambulance, and I hopped in beside him. He had begun to cry and I tried to soothe him on the short ride to the hospital. By the time he was assessed and admitted, my mind was racing with thoughts of Keely. I had left her sitting in the middle of the living room floor, and despite the fact that Keely was almost nine-years-old, she was helpless. *Was Jay able to wake Willard? Would Willard find someone to watch Keely and come to the hospital?* As soon as I could, I phoned him and he answered saying Keely was fine.

"Is Kevan okay?" he asked.

"He'll be fine, but will be in a cast," I said, longing to hear words of comfort.

"Why was he crossing the street alone?" I knew then that there would be no comforting words coming my way from Willard. Tears stung my eyes as I hung up and returned to Kevan's room.

Kevan was in the hospital for a week in traction and came home in a body cast that had to remain on him for six weeks. He had a tutor who came to the house every school day so he didn't fall behind in his work. The church, our family, neighbors and friends reached out to Kevan by sending cards and visiting him. He was so excited that many of his cards had money in them that totaled over $500.

Keely's love for her brother was touching to watch. She knew Kevan was hurt and in her own way, tried to show she cared by sitting as close to him as she possibly could.

I called the guidance office and told the counselor I wouldn't be returning to class to work on my GED and explained the situation. Once again I was unable to "graduate" with my class—not even a GED!

Several weeks later, the guidance counselor called me to ask how Kevan was doing and to let me know the GED exam was being offered the following Saturday. With the extra responsibility I had with Kevan's injury, I had completely forgotten about the GED class.

"I don't think I remember enough to take the

exam," I told him.

"Claudette, you should come and take it anyway. With your life experience, you could probably pass the exam."

"Are you serious?" I asked.

"At least give it a try," he said.

"Well, okay, if you think I have a shot at passing it."

The exam took several hours and I left feeling unsure about many of the answers. Nevertheless, in a week or so, the counselor called.

"Well, didn't I tell you, Claudette? You passed."

"I did?" I gasped at the news. "Did everybody in the class pass the test?"

"No, not everybody. Congratulations! You're officially a high school graduate."

Caring for Kevan and Keely, both completely dependent on me, became more than I could bear. Willard helped as much as he could, but working and sleeping consumed most of his time.

Emotionally and physically, I was falling apart. I felt like Willard blamed me for the accident and, while no one openly accused me, I felt like everyone was secretly blaming me. I even blamed myself. I slogged through the days feeling hopelessly alone.

In desperation, I phoned my sister and told her I felt like taking my life. "I'm sorry, Claudie. I know you have so many problems." I hung up feeling like I had fallen in a dark hole and couldn't climb out. I wanted someone to make everything better. I wanted my mother. *Why, Lord? Isn't it enough that you took my mother and gave me a retarded child? Now, Kevan?*

I made an appointment with my doctor and told him I felt like I couldn't go on and he prescribed a medication for me. When I came home, I took a pill. For the remainder of the day, I felt groggy and lightheaded. It was difficult to put one foot in front of the other, much less take care of the children. I tossed the remainder in the trash. I couldn't and wouldn't live on pills.

From then on, I knew my strength to cope would have to come from God. I would not be able to count on others to fully comprehend my situation or assume they would be there to pitch in and help. On occasion, they may do that, and I would be grateful, but I could not count on anybody. The thought was sobering. It had to be me.

I began to memorize Scripture and even placed

the Bible under my pillow each night. I guess I thought the words would seep through my pillow into my spirit. I prayed my way through the days. My brothers and sisters began stopping in and lending a hand, and gradually I grew stronger. Thankfully, Kevan was healing. I looked forward to the day when the cast would come off.

The more people were around us, the more they saw the distance between Willard and me. However, I still had hope that one day our marriage would grow stronger.

Finally, the day came when the cast came off, and Kevan was well and strong once again. I thanked God for my son whom he spared and for guiding me through one of the most difficult periods of my life.

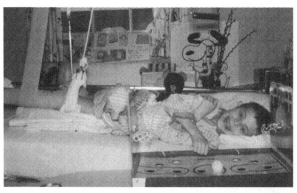

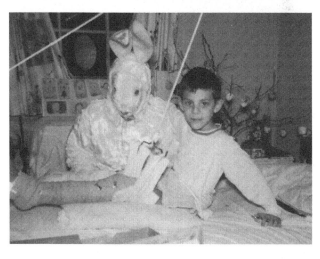

The Voice

Ebony clouds rolling in
Looming, invading my life with sadness
Difficult, hopeless days of despair
And a faint, muted voice calling-
"Walk my way, child."

Desperate days, passing by
Clouded with muddled thoughts
Riddled with sorrow
And yet a voice, louder now-
"Walk my way, child."

Beckoning light, softly illuminating
The hopeless darkness
Hand outstretched, gently pleading
And still the piercing repetition of that voice-
"Walk my way, child."
And I did.

By Eva C. Maddox

Chapter Eighteen

Baseball and Betty

Dividing my time between my two children was demanding and exhausting. However, I was determined to be the best possible mother I could be, refusing to allow Keely with her constant need of attention, overshadow my son. I enrolled Kevan in summer camps and vacation Bible school, and made sure that his time at home with his friends was fun and exciting.

When I saw an advertisement in the local paper for Little League, I signed him up. Thankfully, Willard showed interest in supporting the idea of Kevan playing baseball.

I'll never forget the first time he stepped up to the plate to bat. I was so proud of him I thought my heart would burst wide open. When the pitcher threw the ball, Kevan bit his lip and pulled back to swing and missed. I could hear Willard, who was standing with some of the other dads, coaching him. "Keep your eye on the ball, Kevan!" he shouted. When the second pitch came, Kevan was ready. He slammed the ball and ran as fast as his little legs could carry him to first base.

I picked up Keely and shouted, "Yea! Run Kevan, run!" Keely giggled. She loved the excitement.

Wherever I took Keely, she drew the attention of both adults and children. At age nine, she drooled, walked unsteadily and giggled inappropriately. It was no different at Kevan's baseball games. There were usually children playing around and under the bleachers who would make faces and imitate her behavior. Even though it hurt my feelings, I would smile and try to ignore them. Rarely would adults or children come right out and ask me about Keely. That's why the day Betty Barndt plopped down beside me on the bleachers, I was more than a little surprised.

"Hi, I'm Betty Barndt," she said smiling at me and Keely. I introduced us and pointed out Kevan to her. She had a son playing Little League as well and before I knew it, we were engaged in conversation as if we had known each other for years. Betty was a beautiful person, inside and out. What amazed me most about her was that she appeared completely comfortable with Keely from the start.

During the course of our conversation, Betty told me she had trusted Jesus as her Savior recently and that led me to invite her to a Bible study I had begun. Little did I know she would actually follow through and come the following week. From then on, we became like sisters.

One day, Betty called to say she was coming over to take Keely home with her for a few hours to give me some time to myself. I was shocked. Keely was nine years old and having someone take her for no particular reason was overwhelming.

When Betty walked in, I could hardly speak, I was so full of gratitude. I was thankful for the much needed time alone, yes, but for so much more. My heart was touched just knowing that someone actually understood and cared about me, my life, my daughter and my burden. That had always been the cry of my heart and finally it had happened.

When the two of them left, I thanked God for this angel, Betty, who graced my life that day and would do so many days to come.

Betty and me

Keely

Stigma

Families must develop competence in managing uncomfortable social situations (Marshak & Seligman, 1993; Wikler, 1981). Wikler notes that family members may "face hostile stares, judgmental comments, murmurs of pity, and intrusive requests for personal information whenever they accompany their child to the grocery store, on the bus, or to the park." (p.282) She notes further that families with a child with mental retardation are subject to an increase in the number of stressful encounters as the discrepancy between the child's size and mental functioning increases.

It is probably true that the rather positive portrayals of persons with disabilities in films and television have positively affected attitudes. Nevertheless, our present state of knowledge regarding public and professional sentiment about these persons informs us that attitudes continue to be negative. Thus, for some families, stigmatizing attitudes and social ostracism may be added to the other burdens families must bear.

Ordinary Families, Special Children, 2nd ed., ©1997 The Guilford press, pg. 100

Chapter Nineteen

Touched by Fire

As Keely moved through the remainder of her childhood years her progress showed little improvement, even though I continued to reinforce the skills at home that she was working on at school.

Keely did learn some challenging things while attending summer day camps. She managed to stand and throw a basketball and could actually make a basket! She responded to the teens who worked with her with eagerness and delight. They tossed bean bags with her, played Duck, Duck, Goose and encouraged her to walk and run. She also developed an amazing skill that many children tried to copy unsuccessfully—she could twirl a basketball with her fingers! She would place both index fingers on opposite sides of the ball and twirl away, never once dropping the ball.

Interestingly, when I would hand her the ball, she would rotate it and search for the small indentation. That was her starting point. How she could process that concept and develop that skill, but still not be able to put on her coat, was a puzzle to me.

Keely loved the water and enjoyed splashing in the little pool I set up in the yard. Whenever I said the word "pool," she invariably responded with giggles and would shake her hands like a small excited baby.

I often took her to the community pool and would sit with her in the shallow water, while keeping an eye on Kevan swimming in the deep pool and diving off the diving board.

Even though Keely still drooled, had a smaller than normal head and a hand that drooped, she was a beautiful girl. Other children at the pool, however, did not see her as I did. Often they would stop in front of her and stare, saying she was too big for the baby pool. Many children were scared of her and would simply shy away. I had become accustomed to the stares and whispers and was beginning to think it futile to make anyone understand, especially children.

While at the pool on one occasion, I met Sarah Delp. She and I had been introduced a few years ago, but I really didn't actually know her. After chatting for a few minutes, she placed a book in my hand.

"I have a feeling that this book may help you," she said.

I glanced at the interesting title, "Touched by Fire," thanked her and tucked it into my purse.

Later that day, I had a few minutes before preparing dinner and began reading the book. I couldn't put it down.

The book was about the power of the Holy Spirit in a Christian's life. If anyone needed power, I did. There had been little teaching on this subject in my church, and God used this book to open my eyes and heart to a renewed walk with the Lord. I began to pray differently and claim the Spirit's power over my circumstances. I realized for the first time that there was so much more to this Christian life than just being saved. I recommitted my life to the Lord, attended local studies on the gifts of the Spirit, and began reading Christian books on the subject. It was as though I had been born again all over again!

Keely, age 9

Chapter Twenty

Reflexology

Through the years I learned that routine was critical for Keely. When her routine was interrupted, she would cry and bite her right index finger. Consequently, my life had always revolved around Keely's needs.

Because it was easier to have friends in than try and take Keely out, I began entertaining more frequently. My friend, Betty, and her family became regular dinner guests. Thankfully, Willard actually enjoyed their company and occasionally went fishing with Betty's husband. Our families went on a camping trip together one summer and in spite of the fact that we got lost on the way home, we did enjoy ourselves.

Betty and I became inseparable. We shared our hopes, dreams, and disappointments. Whether on a picnic with the kids or for a ride in the country, we enjoyed being together. She became my confidant. She was always there for me, no matter what.

It didn't take her long to see the lack of togetherness between Willard and me. She reminded me to be patient and hope that God would change things. She encouraged me to make my marriage work, and I kept trying, but nothing I did made a difference.

Kevan was well aware of the problems between his parents. Sometimes he would ask me if we were getting a divorce. I always answered him by saying that God would not want that to happen.

Nevertheless, many times I would sit and try to figure out a way to leave Willard. I had no place to go. I knew I couldn't go to my dad's, and I did not have money to live alone. So I stayed and tried and kept trying. I still loved the man I married, but the warmth, companionship and affection I expected in marriage had not happened. I know it was not all Willard's fault, but I was at a loss as to know what to do. I couldn't change who I was and apparently he couldn't change who he was. My marriage had left me unfulfilled as a person, consequently, my friends, family, children and the church became my life. My days were filled with caring for my children, homemaking, visiting parents of retarded children and serving at church. Willard would often complain that I was always at the church or out running somewhere. He was right. I was.

I heard about reflexology from a friend who thought that it might be a way to help Keely with some of her chronic health problems. I called a woman who had been practicing this modality for a number of years and she agreed to train me. After a year, she invited me to go with her to a certification training meeting where I received my Certificate of Foot Reflexology and Massage. I was so thrilled that I had found a way I could help my daughter.

A friend gave me a massage table and I purchased a recliner, two items necessary for practicing reflexology. My brother John agreed to enclose the back porch for me to use as an office. Even though the space was small, I was able to create an atmosphere of warmth and privacy. How full of pride I felt as I hung my certificate on the wall in the year 1970.

As time went on people heard of my ability to apply reflexology and began calling for appointments. Willard was happy to have a little additional income for our always-strained budget. From the beginning, I tried to adhere to the guidelines I learned during my training, especially when it came to the length of time each treatment should take. However, that was a challenge for me because I could easily get involved in a conversation with a client and run overtime. Willard would occasionally remind me to stay on schedule and while I didn't appreciate that at the time, I now know that was a good thing. It taught me to be consistent with each client.

While working on clients, Keely often sat perched on the massage table watching me. Each time a client came in, she would say, "How are you?" in her unique way of vocalizing. She had become good at imitating my greeting tone.

Even though I had learned reflexology in order to help Keely, I was disappointed that she could not tolerate the pressure on her feet, nor could she sit still long enough for me to complete a treatment. However, due to the continuing number of people calling for an appointment, I knew that God was using the practice of reflexology in my life. As I took on more and more clients the income it produced gave me a small sense of freedom. In addition, my clients became my friends.

I wish I could say that Willard and I had

achieved some sense of togetherness, but it wasn't to be. While we lived in the same house and slept in the same bed, we couldn't have been farther apart. My life was outside my marriage. Although, I continued doing everything in my power to make Willard happy and our home a pleasant place, every year that passed, the rift between us grew.

Betty and me

Reflexology is a type of therapy that involves the massaging of the feet to treat and heal an individual's entire body. It is said to be a type of therapy, used to restore the body's natural balance as well as to help maintain its equilibrium. Sometimes, reflexology involves the hands and ears as well as the feet. In most cases, however, only the feet are involved.

Historically, the use of reflexology dates back to ancient China, Egypt, and Greece. However, it wasn't introduced to Western civilizations until the twentieth century, when M.D William Fitzgerald first introduced it to the West. He referred to this type of treatment as zone therapy.

Today, reflexology is used as a therapeutic treatment for a full range of conditions, including back pain, athletic injuries, and severe headaches. This type of therapy is even said to be effective in treating infertility, digestive disorders, hormonal imbalances, and sleep disorders. Furthermore, many believe it to be particularly helpful in the treatment of a full range of stress-related conditions. However, it is not a cure for medical conditions or diseases. Perhaps one of the most important uses of reflexology is for stress relief.

Excerpt from "The Wise Geek" www.wisegeek.com/*what-is-reflexology.htm*

Chapter Twenty-one

Farewell

My Aunt Margaret had always been a source of strength for me. I realized that God had used her in a very special way to teach me about real love and to be an example of love to those around me. I knew Aunt Margaret was not a perfect person, but she was an amazing example of forgiveness, for she understood she had been forgiven.

Aunt Margaret was not serious all the time. She was fun to be around too. I have fond memories of her playing the piano for us on Friday nights. We kids would stand around her and sing as she belted out some hymns and popular tunes of the time.

Everybody in our small community knew Aunt Margaret and many had experienced her kindness.

The day I learned she had breast cancer, I was

devastated, but Aunt Margaret was at peace. She was kind and patient and was always trying to help others even though she knew she was dying. I wasn't the only one who was shocked and grieved upon hearing of her illness. My cousins, my aunts—everyone who knew her was hurting.

As her disease grew worse, I tried to comfort her as much and as often as I could. She only lived a few miles from us in Telford and after supper and the dishes were done, I would jump in the car and drive over to Aunt Margaret's. My heart was grieving but I tried not to let it show in her presence, but she knew anyway. Even when she was near death, she would smile a weak smile at me and squeeze my hand. My heart was ripping apart.

The day of her graveside service, my brothers and sisters and I stood cold, unhappy and feeling a sense of abandonment. Aunt Margaret, the one who had shown us unconditional love lay cold in the ground.

I suffered her loss for years, often breaking into tears without warning. The only thing I knew was that sweet Aunt Margaret was gone. And although I knew I would see her again in heaven one day, my grief was deep and painful.

Beloved Aunt Margaret

Children of <u>Kate A. Barnes and Harvey J. Bossert</u>

- Henry B. Bossert was born 7 OCT 1895 in PA.
- Elva Bossert was born SEP 1898 in PA.
- Catherine B. Bossert was born 26 OCT 1899 in PA.
- Verda B. Bossert was born 5 APR 1912 in PA, and died 9 JUN 1976.
- **Margaret B. Bossert** was born 9 SEP 1913 in Montgomery Co, PA, and died 4 AUG 1967.
- Harvey B. Bossert was born 26 OCT 1916 in Montgomery Co, PA, and died 21 DEC 2006 in (of) Wellsboro, Tioga Co, PA per SSDI.

☐ *Name:* Margaret B. Bossert
☐ *Sex:* F
☐ *Birth:* 9 SEP 1913 in Montgomery Co, PA
☐ *Death:* 4 AUG 1967

Father: <u>Harvey J. Bossert</u> b: 20 APR 1876 in Montgomery Co, PA
Mother: <u>Kate A. Barnes</u> b: 28 SEP 1877 in Montgomery Co, PA

Source: *RootsWeb's WorldConnect Project*

Chapter Twenty-two

Fresh Air

Even though I had a full life, I had a zest for living that kept me pursuing new experiences.

For several summers I signed up to host a Fresh Air child. The Fresh Air program was sponsored by local churches in our community. It was a way to give inner city children an experience of life outside the city. Many of these children came from troubled homes and had behavior problems. Willard was not happy about my involvement with these children and took little interest in them.

Why was I so determined to work with these children? I certainly had enough to do without taking more responsibility. Was it because I knew what it was like to be a child crying out for attention and love? I have no answer. I only know God used me in the lives of several of the Fresh Air children.

The first Fresh Air child to come to our home was Althea, a six-year-old girl. When Kevan and Althea went out to play on the swing set, I caught a glimpse of our next door neighbor staring out her kitchen window, but when I smiled and waved, she turned away.

Summer evenings in our row home neighborhood found residents sitting on their front porches where we called to one another with neighborly greetings. However, when Althea and other Fresh Air children appeared on our front porch, I sensed an undercurrent of gossip. Although it bothered me, I did my best to ignore them.

Keely loved all the Fresh Air kids and they loved her and treated her with kindness. She loved to feel their hair and they patiently allowed her to run her fingers through it and giggle.

Kevan, too, got along well with all the children I hosted. He was glad to have someone to play with. Once in a while some neighborhood children would poke fun at them, and Kevan was quick to become their defender.

I certainly had my challenges with all the kids.

One was their colorful language that shocked Kevan. I had to explain to him what kind of homes these children came from and he accepted them as they were.

One child was a bed-wetter and hid his wet underwear under the mattress until the odor gave him away. These children came with all kinds of emotional problems, and I spent time listening and encouraging each one.

No matter how I tried to get people to warm up to them and accept them, it didn't happen. One family member, upon seeing Althea for the first time, suggested I might be exposing my family to lice. I decided to wash Althea's just to be sure. I dribbled the shampoo over her hair and scrubbed until I was sure her scalp would bleed. When she jumped out of the tub, I towel-dried her hair, but I had trouble copying the neat little braids she had arrived with. I thought perhaps Vaseline would help and that just made a sticky mess. Althea soon tired of me messing with her hair, so I smoothed it down the best I could and pulled it into a pony tail of sorts. At least she didn't have lice.

After three summers of hosting Fresh Air kids and not feeling Willard's support about it, I decided it had become too much for me and I gave up.

I am confident, though, that God will honor the seeds of love sown in their hearts as I shared Jesus with each child.

Two Fresh Air Program girls and me

Keely and Althea

Chapter Twenty-three

A Difficult Decision

I had been taking Keely to Dr. Thomas for monthly exams for years. As he finished the exam just prior to Keely's 13th birthday, Dr. Thomas asked me to step into his office to discuss a matter. As usual, my heart flipped in my chest. I couldn't help but press him for an answer before we could leave the exam room.

"What is it, doctor? Is something else wrong?"

"Just take Keely into my office and have a seat. I'll be right there," he said.

"Let's go, Keely," I said, trying to keep my mood light. Keely could sense mood changes in me and would respond accordingly. If I were sad or angry, she would burst into tears, but if I kept my tone happy, she would be happy too.

Dr. Thomas took his seat behind his desk, removed his glasses and smiled at me. I felt like I needed to shake him to spill what was on his mind, but I forced a smile in return.

"Claudette, have you given any thought as to how you will handle Keely's periods when they begin?"

I couldn't believe it had never crossed my mind. I suppose it was because Keely was still such a little girl. He was right! How *would* I handle that? I stumbled over my words as I confessed I had no plans.

"If you wish, I could recommend a surgeon."

"Are you suggesting Keely have a hysterectomy?" I was shocked.

"Only you can make that decision, Claudette, but I think you should at least think about it. In addition, I want you to be very careful who Keely is alone with. She is a sweet, loving girl and is vulnerable when it comes to sexual abuse. Because she cannot tell you when something happens to her, she could be taken advantage of and you would never know it."

The thought of Keely being raped filled me with fear. *Who would do such a thing?*

On the drive home, I rehearsed the males in Keely's life—ones she might be alone with. The workers at Keely's daycare program were females, but that didn't mean there wouldn't be males involved in her programs some day. *One more thing to worry about.*

When I got home, I discussed with Willard what Dr. Thomas had suggested regarding a hysterectomy for Keely. He couldn't believe I was actually considering putting Keely through an operation. Others offered their opinions as well. However, I began thinking about how I would handle Keely if she began menstruation. It only took me two days to make a decision. I called Dr. Winn, the surgeon that Dr. Thomas recommended, and scheduled an appointment.

Two weeks before the surgery, Keely had her first period. I couldn't believe it! I found her in a mess and needed no other confirmation that I had made the right decision.

I packed my suitcase and took Keely to Grand View Hospital for her surgery. I would be staying with her the entire time, leaving Kevan in the care of Willard.

Keely's surgery went well and she returned to the pediatric floor looking pale and weak. Carolyn Bergey came to the hospital and sat and prayed with me, and I was so happy to have her encouragement. I know Betty came to visit too, as well as family members, but I was so focused on Keely's care that I have little recollection of them.

One morning a group of medical students came into Keely's room and one young man presumed to ask me a personal question.

"Have you considered that this surgery your daughter has had may impact her negatively in the future?"

I felt anger start in my toes and burn its way to my cheeks. "You know what?" I asked. "I think it's time for you guys to leave," I said, holding the door open for them. They filed out, heads lowered, mumbling an apology. *Why did a student who didn't know anything about Keely or me, feel free to ask that kind of personal question?*

Even though the med student had angered me, he succeeded in creating doubt in my mind. Had I made the right decision? Would Keely suffer in some unknown way in the future because of the surgery? Maybe Willard was right. Maybe I shouldn't have put her through it.

Keely had lost weight and was still very weak

and pale when we left the hospital three weeks after the surgery. When we arrived home, I had so many things to handle that all doubts of my decision to have Keely undergo a hysterectomy vanished.

Chapter Twenty-four

Sunday Morning Crisis

I suppose I should have become somewhat accustomed to crises, but nothing could have prepared me for what happened next. It was a Sunday morning and Willard had gone for his annual deer hunting trip in the mountains several hours away. I had bathed and dressed Keely and placed her on the sofa so I could finish getting ready for church. I ran upstairs, told Kevan to hurry in the shower, and I was changing clothes when a shrill scream exploded through the house. I raced down the steps in sheer panic. Keely lay on her back with blood gushing from her right eye.

I screamed for Kevan, grabbed a dishtowel and dropped down beside Keely. My hands were shaking and I felt nausea roaring in my throat as I placed the towel over Keely's eye to stop the bleeding. Kevan had bolted down the steps, and I instructed him to hold the towel in place while I called the hospital.

"I'm Claudette Price and my daughter has injured her eye. She is bleeding profusely and I'm on my way there." I had blurted the words so fast I only hoped they made sense.

Kevan and I managed to get Keely into the car and we headed for the hospital. Waves of panic swept through me. My hands were shaking so badly, I could scarcely control the car. I knew I needed someone besides Kevan to help me or I wouldn't even make it to the hospital. I headed for Leidy's UCC Church.

"Mom, where are you going?" asked Kevan. "This isn't the way to the hospital." He was trying to be brave, but I could hear the panic in his voice.

"I'm going to get Betty," I said, barely able to speak. I knew she would be at her church.

"Run in and tell Aunt Betty to come and help!" Kevan dashed inside and seconds later Betty came flying out with Kevan. She squeezed into the front seat beside Keely as Kevan dove into the back. Betty's presence seemed to prop me up and her calm confidence enabled me to drive the rest of the way to the hospital without totally losing it.

After Keely was admitted, I phoned Willard to tell him what had happened.

"Willard, you have to come home. Keely has had an accident," I blurted. I longed to hear concern and compassion from him.

"What do you mean? What kind of accident?"

"It's her eye. She's bleeding from her eye, Willard. I don't know what happened. You need to come home."

"Well, I can't just come home. I just got here and it's a three hour drive."

"Willard, Keely may lose her eye. It's hemorrhaging badly. You're her father and you should be here."

"Well, what happened to her? She was fine when I left." I wanted to scream into the phone, but as calmly as I could I tried explaining.

"I'm not sure what happened. I only know her eye is bleeding and she may have to have surgery."

"Well, I can't come home till Wednesday."

"Fine. Come home when you come home."

I hung up as tears filled my eyes. True to his Word, he arrived on Wednesday.

The doctors questioned me to try and determine

what punctured Keely's eye. They needed to know if glass or splinters or some other object may still be in her eye. At the time I found her on the floor, I was in such a panic that I didn't take time to look around. I returned to the house to examine the living room to see what I could find. That's when I discovered the corner of our wooden hutch was covered in blood. Keely had tripped on the rug and fallen forward into the hutch, her eye taking the brunt of the fall.

Returning to the hospital with what I had discovered, the doctors focused on stabilizing Keely and trying to avoid surgery to remove the eye, knowing that she would not be able to handle having a prosthetic eye. I stayed by her side day and night until she was able to come home. It took six weeks. All of the blood still had not been absorbed from the injured eye when she left the hospital, but she was stable enough to go home. She had lost all vision in that eye.

Keely could not open either eye for a number of months, then slowly, with lots of encouragement, she began opening her good eye. Keely had several people who came and tried to get her to open her eye and be responsive. Lola Huntsinger, Keely's teacher, came and tried to get her to eat and open her eye by teasing her.

I am so grateful for those who took their time to visit Keely and encourage me during those difficult days. I do remember some of them. Cindy Longacre was one. She had been a volunteer at Keely's summer camp and had begun stopping by the house. She grew close to both Kevan and Keely. When Keely had the eye accident, she would drop by after school and sit with Keely, teasing her and trying to encourage her to open her good eye. Other friends and family came— Carolyn Bergey and, of course, Betty; John and Marty, Polly and Art, Daddy and Beulah and many others in my family came as well.

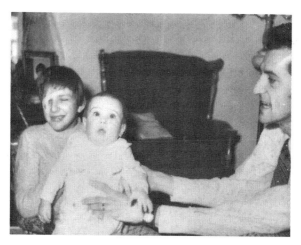

My brother, John, helping Keely hold his baby daughter

Keely was listless and emotionally closed and had no appetite for a long time. She was not the same bubbly, happy Keely.

I had several people question me about the fall. "Was she in her stocking feet? Was she alone?"

Of course, I blamed myself for a time, but I knew I had always been very careful with Keely and with God's help, I refused to burden myself with guilt. I had more than enough to deal with.

I was blessed to meet the new director of education at Zion Mennonite, Hedy Sawadsky, who dropped by one day during Keely's convalescence. Hedy was a soft-spoken, peace advocate and a gentle, loving woman. She touched my life with such compassion.

Hedy and me

"Oh Claudette, you really have a burden here. Do you have a support team?"

Support team? While I had visitors, there was no *team* who helped carry the burdens I carried. Just hearing Hedy say those words and knowing she understood, brought tears to my eyes.

Hedy and I grew to be close friends. She introduced me to prayer and fasting on a deeper level. She and I often prayed together and when she moved back to Canada some years later, it left a huge hole in my heart. Nevertheless, we remain lifelong friends.

Willard never opened his heart to my friends, choosing to avoid them when they came to the house. However, he did love Keely, and spent time with her whenever he wasn't working.

It took about a year before Keely became accustomed to seeing with one eye. She began walking slowly and cautiously, and I realized she would never be the same Keely. Prior to her accident, Keely would usually jump excitedly from where she was seated and dart across the room which meant she often bumped into things and had minor bruises. The eye injury had slowed her down. Years later I would realize the truth of Romans 8:28, "All things work together for good for those who love God, who are called according to his purpose." How could my child losing her eye possibly be a good thing? Losing sight in her eye slowed Keely down. That meant she was less likely to suffer more serious accidents, and it enabled me to keep pace with her as I aged. I had met a number of retarded children who were so active and a handful for their parents. I wouldn't wish the accident on Keely, of course, but I believe there is good in everything if we only take time to look for it.

Keely returned to school after several months of recuperation. I knew she would be fine under Lola's loving protection and training.

Chapter Twenty-five

A New Church

The church we attended was not an evangelistic church. I knew that I had come to Christ because someone explained to me that I needed a Savior, and if I died without Christ in my heart, I would be destined for hell. It troubled me that the Word of God wasn't made clear regarding salvation at our church. I wasn't even sure my own husband was a true believer. *Had he ever really been saved?* Our minister certainly preached good sermons, but he never had an altar call following his sermons—at least while I was there.

My brother, John, and his wife Marty had joined an independent Baptist Church in the area and began talking to me about how much they enjoyed it. They even enrolled their children in the Christian academy.

One Sunday, I decided to go visit the services to see what it was all about.

My experience there was very much like the one I experienced at my friend Carolyn's church where I accepted Christ. The sermon was based on the prodigal son and the message of repentance and forgiveness was clear and direct. The people were friendly and appeared excited about their faith. I was convinced God wanted my family to worship there.

I couldn't wait to share my thoughts with Willard. I wanted to make sure he was saved. I wanted us to be a real family and for Willard to be the spiritual head of our family. I was sure all this would happen if we became part of this church.

"Willard, what do you think about us attending the church where John and Marty have been going? They really like it."

"What's wrong with our church?" he asked.

"I would just like to try a different church." I didn't want to have to explain my doubts about his salvation.

"Well, I guess so," he said. He seemed to have no opinion at all about it. I was surprised he agreed so readily, but I was glad. I was hoping that joining a more fundamental church would make a difference in Willard. He would grow and ultimately our marriage would grow too.

One Sunday morning following the sermon, the pastor issued an invitation for anyone to come forward who would like to become part of the church. Willard and I went forward with Kevan and Keely. Later we met with the pastor and deacons and were all four immersed and became members.

Shortly after joining, I learned that there was a Sunday school class for retarded children and adults and was excited to have Keely become part of it. Keely loved the class and when I went to pick her up, she was always well cared for and happy.

It was difficult for Kevan to make a church switch at this time in his life because it meant leaving the friends he had grown up with. However, he made the best of it, but was never really happy in the new youth group.

One Sunday morning I was sitting in church with a friend waiting for the service to start when I overheard a lady in front of us talking about diets. I tapped her on the shoulder and introduced myself, and we talked briefly about losing weight. I learned she was

Eva Bosh, a teacher in the church academy. Little did I know it then, but she was to become one of my closest and dearest friends.

John and Marty Bossert

Chapter Twenty-six

Called to Action

Keely was almost eighteen when I received a call from her social worker, Bill Swartzendruber, asking me to come in for a consultation. I was always glad to get feedback from the people who worked with Keely, so I sailed into his office with excitement.

"Mrs. Price, as you know Keely will be turning eighteen soon, and we need to look into signing her up for Social Security Disability Insurance."

"Oh, I don't think that will be necessary," I said. "Keely will be staying with us at home." I was proud and confident that we could take care of Keely's needs all by ourselves. We certainly didn't need charity!

"Mrs. Price, it is critical for you to access all the financial aid available for Keely. She can get help through Social Security as well as Montgomery County and the State of Pennsylvania. You may not be able to meet all her needs as you grow older. Also, as Keely ages she will need care-givers and special equipment and that will cost a great deal of money. We need to take into consideration what is best for her both now and in the future."

Needless to say, we signed Keely up for SSI.

As we continued to converse, I shared my concerns about all the retarded children and their parents in our area—so many of them needed help. Ever since Keely was a baby, I had been involved with these parents and their children to some degree, and my heart went out to them as I watched them struggle year after year.

"Bill, these families are really hurting. Many of the parents are getting older and are still trying to care for their severely handicapped children at home. Other than state institutions, there are simply no local facilities for them."

"I realize that, Claudette. What do you think we can do about it?"

"I think we need a home right here; a place where parents can place their kids and still be close enough to them to keep connected."

"You are absolutely right, Claudette. Let's get the ball rolling. Why don't you call some of the parents, and we'll arrange a meeting to discuss the issue."

I was elated that Bill was willing to at least *discuss* the issue. I knew in my heart it could be done. Since Keely's birth, through hard work, community projects and education, I had seen people's attitudes toward the mentally handicapped begin to change. However, much more was needed, but I knew that change takes time. I prayed that God would give me the wisdom, strength and courage to plunge into this new venture. I was sure the idea of getting involved in another project would not set well with Willard, but I couldn't let that stop me. After all, who knows what the future held for Keely. Would she have to be in a facility someday? Would we always be able to care for her at home? It seemed almost every year that went by, Keely had another health crisis.

I pulled out my address book and started phoning parents. I called the Ledrocks, Bernotes's, Brazicks, the Yerks and some others. I knew each of these families well and they all had a severely handicapped child, and they were more than happy to come to a meeting. They were dealing with extremely difficult circumstances at home and some were barely holding on.

Our first meeting was held on May 31, 1974, at Penn Foundation in Sellersville, Pennsylvania. The discussion was lively and a spirit of hope invaded the large all-purpose room. That was the first of many meetings that would later lead to the formation of Community Foundation for Human Development, Incorporated. The Foundation included a number of business and professional people, and eventually a board of directors was formed. I recall Elyse Fox and Dorothy Garis with Grand View Hospital, being a huge part of the planning process and, of course, Bill Swartzendruber. There were many others whose names now escape me, but they were all instrumental in those critical planning stages.

I served on the board of Community Foundation and as chairman of the parent group, now a separate entity from the Foundation. There were so many things Community Foundation had to consider. There were zoning laws, contracts, costs, fund-raising and a myriad of other issues to be decided. Fortunately, Grand View Hospital donated land for the building at a cost of

$1.00. The facility would be built on several acres behind the hospital, an ideal location.

All the meetings and all the work finally paid off when Ridge Crest, the name chosen for the residential facility, became a reality. I will never forget the open house. Ridge Crest was a beautiful building with lovely decorated bedrooms. My heart swelled with pride at what God had accomplished. Community Foundation would eventually begin a day care center for handicapped individuals as well as a number of group homes.

Kevan and Keely

The History of Ridge Crest

LifePath, formerly the Community Foundation for Human Development, was started in 1974 by a group of parents from the Pennridge area who wanted more individualized care for their special needs children. LifePath's dedicated pediatric facility, Ridge Crest, was opened in Sellersville as a place where medically-fragile and technology-dependent children and their families could find the help they needed. Soon after, residential housing was established for adults with developmental disabilities as the transition from institutionalization to community-based supports continued. LifePath's programs and services revolved around one common theme — to provide individuals with the highest quality care possible in an environment of unconditional love, respect and dignity.

Excerpt from LifePath website:
http://www.lifepath.org/aboutus.html Used by permission

Chapter Twenty-seven

Another Challenge

My sister-in-law, Marty, called me one day to tell me about a Vietnamese family who really needed help. She thought that I might consider volunteering to assist them. I took a deep breath and wondered if I should take on another challenge. Marty said they lived right down the street from me, so it would be convenient to work with them. The family of six had just arrived in the states and they could not speak a word of English.

I decided that I would at least drop in and introduce myself. After my first visit with them, I knew God was calling me to pitch in and do what I could to help this family.

The Lutheran church had provided them with a sparsely furnished apartment and helped the father get a

job at the local poultry plant. I'm not sure what else the church did for them, but the more involved I became with the family, the more needs they seemed to have.

I began taking items such as a toaster, waste baskets and dish towels each time I visited. I took them to buy clothing and food, taught them English and raised $750 so they could purchase a used car. I gave them my phone number and told them to call me if they needed me. Often the phone would ring and there would be total silence on the other end. I knew from their silence that they needed me, so I would jump in the car and run to their house.

If Keely was not in school, and Willard was at work, Keely would come along with me. She always laughed around them probably because of the way they spoke. The sounds they made were so different from what she was used to. The Vietnamese were always kind and loving to Keely.

There were many instances when I had to deal with difficult situations with them. On one occasion they called me because a milkman was at their door trying to explain what milk delivery was. Coming from Vietnam, they had no idea what this man was trying to tell them about milk. When I arrived, I managed to explain milk delivery in America to them.

They had so many needs that at times I was completely overwhelmed and felt as though I was in Vietnam myself. I soon learned it was not a give and take friendship but a give and give. What I thought was going to be an English lesson turned into an all-consuming involvement.

I did not tell Willard everything I did for them to avoid confrontation.

I had grown close to their young daughter, Nhuam, often having her over to our home. I would have talks with her about Jesus, and one day she prayed and invited Him into her heart. Nhuam was a special little girl whose love for Jesus grew in the few short years she had on this earth.

On a visit to the family one day, I found her in bed. She had had a seizure. I gathered her up and took her immediately to the hospital. Nhuam was diagnosed with a brain tumor. She lived two years after her diagnosis. I made many trips to Children's Hospital in Philadelphia to visit Nhuam and tried to encourage her parents. I was confident Nhuam knew the Lord, for she talked to me about Him often. Her parents gave her a Christian burial saying, "Nhuam was not a Buddhist like us."

My involvement with the Vietnamese family was stressful and draining, and many of my friendships began to suffer because I was all-consumed by the needs of the Nugyen family. John and Marty understood what a difficult ministry it was because they too, worked with a Vietnamese family and we often shared the challenges it presented.

Eventually, I knew I had done all I could and should do to help this family become established in this country. If I continued to play the role of provider, problem-solver, and counselor, they would not be forced to stand on their own two feet. They now had a car, a home, furniture, jobs and could speak limited English. It was time for them to make their lives work.

In addition, I later learned that they had been receiving help from the government all along. I was disappointed and felt somewhat "used" when I heard that, but I was at peace knowing I had done the right thing by helping them. Now I needed to focus on my own life.

Needless to say, my work with this family drove a bigger wedge between Willard and me. He did not approve of my work with them, did not once go to visit or help in any way. I realized by then, I would never be able to expect Willard to support or understand my interests or involvements.

The end of the Vietnam War prompted millions to flee the country escaping from the new Communist regime and Communists from the North. Being an international humanitarian crisis, six countries accepted Vietnamese refugees and these were the United States, Canada, Great Britain, France, West Germany, and Australia.

from: Wikipedia, the free encylcpedia

Nhuam

Death leaves a heartache no one can heal,
Love leaves a memory no one can steal.
-from a headstone in Ireland

Chapter Twenty-eight

Unexpected Friendship

I was hoping our move to a different church would encourage Willard to get involved, but he wasn't interested in any of the church activities other than Sunday morning worship. I had always pushed for him to become the spiritual head of our home. The church encouraged us to have a family altar, and I bought devotional magazines and tried to get Willard to lead our family in worship time, but it didn't happen. I suppose he wasn't comfortable with the concept so I dropped the idea.

When the pastor announced there would be a weekend marriage retreat, I asked Willard if we could go. When he agreed, I asked Marty to sit with Keely, and we made plans to attend.

It was never easy for me to find a sitter for

Keely, so I was blessed when Marty or Betty were able to help, even though they both worked full time and had families of their own.

The marriage retreat was interesting and offered good information, but Willard was not responsive to the ideas they brought up. *Why are we here?* I couldn't wait to get home to Keely. The last few hours dragged by.

On our way from one class session to another, I was tired and bored as I walked behind Willard. I glanced up to see Don and Eva Bosh passing us on their way to another class. I remember thinking that she didn't look any happier than I felt.

Not long after that retreat, I heard that Don had walked out on Eva and their four children. Marty and I took some food over to the small apartment she had moved into, not far from where we lived in Souderton. Over the next few months, we became close friends as we both shared our life stories of hurts and heartbreaks.

As I relayed the story of my life with Keely to Eva, she was genuinely interested in hearing, helping and supporting my efforts. Our hearts were drawn together in friendship.

Looking back on how our relationship began, I

understand now that both of us had an enormous need to be heard and understood. In spite of our busy lives we managed to spend hours together talking and listening, talking and listening.

In addition, after so many years of giving to everyone else, I believe I was near a breaking point in my life. I was exhausted, and felt like everyone wanted something from me. I couldn't seem to say "no." I bent over backwards to help whoever called, consequently, I was completely drained emotionally and sapped of energy. It seemed that only Eva understood and didn't want something from me.

I begged Willard to take me somewhere. I needed to get away— to go on a vacation.

"Willard, we've never gone away together. Do you realize that? In twenty-one years of marriage, we have never gotten a sitter and gone anywhere!"

"Don't be ridiculous, Claudie. There's no money for a vacation."

"Well, borrow the money. It will be worth it," I said.

"Don't talk so silly. We can't just up and go on a trip." He dismissed my pleas and continued reading the newspaper.

Excerpt from: *Married with Disabled Children;* by Marie Hartwell-Walker, Ed.D, Dec. 10, 2006; See complete article: http://psychcentral.com/lib/2006/married-with-disabled-children/

Can this marriage survive? It's a question many of us ask as we try to juggle the care of a disabled child, the needs of our other children, and, oh yes, the relationship to that person I'm married to. The good news is that marriages with a disabled child are no more likely to end in divorce than others.

In the case of marriages with disabled children, there are some unique variables. A disabled child is a child with multiple needs. Parenting a disabled child usually involves learning about and dealing with multiple specialists, multiple systems, and multiple expenses that parents of typical children never have to even think about. Learning about the disability, providing daily care, choosing treatment options, managing a complex medical system, negotiating insurance, advocating for special needs schooling and responding to the legitimate needs of other family members adds another full-time job to the family mix.

Tips for being a successful married team:

- Communicate. Communicate. Communicate
- Make a clear decision about who does what
- Figure out how you will deal with reduced finances
- Recognize that things don't have to be the same to be "fair"
- Go out of the way to comfort and reassure each other
- Make room for everyone to have and express feelings
- You don't have to go it alone
- There's no one right way to do it

Chapter Twenty-nine

A Big Move

After Ridge Crest was completed, I continued to meet with some of the parents who were part of the original group that initiated the talks leading to the formation of Community Foundation. Several of them had placed their children (now adults) in Ridge Crest.

When I visited Ridge Crest, I was impressed by the pleasant patient rooms. Great care had been taken to decorate them to look comfortable and homey. Strolling through the facility, again I was overcome with gratefulness for such a fantastic facility right here in our community. What a blessing!

More importantly was the professional and tender way the staff interacted with the patients as they followed each child's individualized care plan.

Keely was eighteen and still had not mastered self-help concepts. In addition, I knew I had pampered and protected her way too much. I began thinking that perhaps Keely would benefit being separated from me and experience more intense training that Ridge Crest was promoting. Maybe they could do what I and others had failed to do.

I called Bill Swartzendruber and asked him if he thought Keely would progress in the Ridge Crest program, and he readily agreed. He told me to put in an application and there would be a spot for her.

I spoke with Willard about my thoughts, and he was totally opposed to the idea. Nevertheless, without his input, I made application, and Keely was accepted into the program. I know I didn't respect Willard's wishes, but I had Keely's best interest at heart. For eighteen years, I had been forced to make all the decisions regarding her care, so why would this decision be any different?

I had no intention of placing Keely permanently, but to see if she could gain more skills than she had acquired thus far. I labeled her clothing, packed her bag and prepared to make the most difficult journey I would ever make. Keely was moving out.

Kevan accompanied Keely and me to Ridge Crest and was a great comfort as I signed the papers and got Keely settled in her new home. I was happy to know that I could visit her any time I wanted.

Kevan had always stood by my side as though he were Keely's father. Many evenings after Willard had gone to bed, the two of us would walk downtown to the local pizza parlor and talk about changes in our family. He had lots of friends and would share his experiences with me, and I would share my feelings about Keely with him. By this time he was well aware of the problems between his father and me. I told him I had been trying for years to get his dad to agree to go with me for marriage counseling, but had been unsuccessful.

"More than likely, Kevan, we will be separating," I told him.

"If you leave Dad, I'm going with you, Mom," Kevan vowed.

"You should stay with your father, Kevan. He will help you and stick by you."

"No, Mother. You are the one who has always been there for me. Where you go, I will go."

"Kevan, no matter what happens, you need to

always remember he is your father and you need to respect him. It's not that he is a bad person. He isn't. It's just that we are so completely different." I wasn't sure Kevan really believed I would ever leave because he knew how I felt about divorce, but it looked as though it was inevitable.

With Kevan's life full of work, friends and his car, and Keely at Ridge Crest, the problems in our marriage came more into focus. I had already given up on trying to get Willard to understand me, but I still hoped he would agree to counseling.

As the weeks wore on, I felt myself giving up. Even though I knew it was wrong, I felt I had to make changes. But what could I do? I had very little money saved from reflexology. That's when I decided I would look for a job.

I applied to a local nursing home and was hired for the night shift. It had been many years since I had worked outside the home, so it was quite an adjustment for me. In addition, I managed to maintain a small reflexology clientele.

I enjoyed my job working with the patients at the nursing home, doing my best to bring joy into their lives by singing to them, speaking Pennsylvania Dutch and massaging their feet. I made friends with the staff too, enjoying the camaraderie we shared.

On top of working full time, I picked up Keely on Wednesdays and brought her home for the night. No matter how exhausted I felt, I was driven to get her, knowing she needed me. Every Friday night, I picked her up again for the weekend and returned her to Ridge Crest on Sunday evening. It was a grueling schedule, but I was determined to do what I thought was best for my daughter.

Our marriage had completely broken down. I begged Willard time and again to go for counseling, but he always refused, saying it was me who needed counseling and not him.

I had never been what you would call an angry person. For years I had swallowed my feelings and tolerated Willard's silences, his lack of interest in me, his disdain of my friends and just about everything I did. I never measured up in his eyes. I was tired of living like that. All the emotions I had felt and never allowed to surface came surging up. I became an angry woman, once even resorting to slapping Willard when he accused me of being a lousy wife and mother. After that I knew I had to leave. I had to get out.

A search on Amazon.com for books on marriage, revealed 13,327 currently available. Of those, 1,027 were Christian books.

Approximately 37% of <u>Christian</u> marriages end in divorce. If you are married and are looking for some helpful resources for your own marriage, I have listed 5 of the best-selling Christian books available on marriage.

Sacred Marriage, Gary Thomas

Five Love Languages, Gary Chapman

Every Man's Marriage, Stephen Arterburn

Hidden Keys of a Loving, Lasting Marriage, Gary Smalley

Love & Respect: The Love She Most Desires, the Respect He Desperately Needs, Dr. Emerson Eggerichs

Chapter Thirty

Turning Away

Kevan spent hours hanging out with his friends, and I felt myself missing his companionship. Keely was not adjusting to life at Ridge Crest as I had hoped, and I was worried at her loss of weight and her increasing irritability. The Vietnamese family had drained so much of my energy, and I felt completely alone. I was tired— tired of a loveless marriage, tired of taking on everyone else's troubles and just plain tired from working. It was my fault for allowing this to happen.

I thought nobody except Eva knew the depth of my pain and frustration. I never even told my friend, Betty, who had stood by me through thick and thin. I really regret my actions during those days. I know Betty would have done anything for me, but I shut her out. I know I hurt her deeply. I think I was scared and ashamed. I did what I did and I have no good reasons for it. I spent every spare minute with my friend, Eva, who I felt understood what it was like to have more on your plate than you can handle.

One evening I told Willard I was going to leave him if he didn't go for help. Even though I knew what God's Word said about marriage, I was turning a deaf ear to that truth.

Once again, Willard insisted that it was me who needed to go for help and not him. I was a run-a-round who couldn't sit still. Part of that was true. I did run around. However, that was only because there was nothing at home for me and there never had been. I knew if I sat at home and watched television with him, never had friends in, took telephone calls or volunteered for another committee or project, he would be happy. I couldn't do that. I would die.

Every time we saw one another, we fought and yelled. I made up my mind. I was leaving.

"What will people think if you leave me?"

"I can't control what people think."

Sadness swept over me as I listened to his desperate attempts to keep me there. I knew then, that he never really had loved me. I had done everything I could to try and win his love but I had failed. Even as he continued trying to persuade me not to leave, a part of me wanted him to cry and beg me to stay because he loved me. It didn't happen. Now I just wanted it over.

I called an attorney and made an appointment. I wanted to find out how to obtain a legal separation. I thought that if I just separated from Willard, he might agree to go for help and there might be a chance for us.

"Mrs. Price, take your time and fill me in on why you wanted to see me." The compassion in the lawyer's voice was all I needed for the tears to begin. Years of pent-up feelings poured out of me as though a floodgate had opened. I tried to make him understand the depths of my pain, frustration and turmoil. I was scared to death.

Finally able to gain some composure, I asked about a legal separation. He didn't answer right away, but rather drummed on his desk with his fingers, studied my face and asked, "Are you sure you want to do this?"

I couldn't even answer that question. *Did I want to do this? No! I wanted a husband who loved me and would share my life, but that would never happen with Willard Price.*

"Yes," I answered. "I want out."

"Then I suggest that you pack up and leave Willard while he is at work," he said, "so that you can avoid confrontation." I realize now what foolish advice that was, but I listened to him nevertheless.

I went to see my dad at his job and asked him if he would consider co-signing a loan for me.

"Why do you need a loan," he asked.

"Daddy, I'm going to leave Willard." He took my arm and led me to a place where we could sit down.

"Now why would you want to leave your husband, Claudie?"

"Our marriage has never been good, Daddy, and I'm tired of trying to make it work. There is nothing between us anymore. Can't you help me out? I'll pay you back."

After studying my face for a few minutes, he said, "I'll talk it over with Beulah and get back to you." He called in a day or two and went to the bank with me and co-signed a loan for $500.

I called Eva and told her I was leaving Willard. She wasn't shocked but her voice was full of concern.

"Do you think Kevan and I can stay with you until I can find a place of my own?" I asked.

"You know you're welcome," she said, "but it's a small apartment and we'll be jammed in here. I hope you know what you're doing, Claudie. This is a huge decision you're making."

"I know that. I just need you to say we can come. We'll make it work. I'll get a place as soon as I can."

She agreed and then I called some friends who said they would help me move and store my furniture in their home until I could find an apartment.

While Willard was at work, we loaded everything on a truck except the bare essentials that Willard would need. They drove away and Kevan and I went to Eva's.

Of course, hindsight being so much sharper, I realize I was wrong, and if I could go back and do things differently, I certainly would. I had no real grounds for divorce. Everything I've stated about my feelings is true, but they don't add up to Biblical grounds for leaving Willard. I transgressed God's law and later I would understand the seriousness of my sin. Even leaving the way I did, while Willard was at work, seems cruel and rather ridiculous now. But that was then and that was how it played out.

I am so grateful that I serve a forgiving and merciful God. How I praise Him for His faithful love that never wavers in spite of my own unfaithfulness!

Chapter Thirty-one

New Beginnings

Kevan and I stayed with Eva for a couple of months until an apartment opened on the first floor of the same building. Keely was still in Ridge Crest, and I continued to bring her home as often as possible. Following the separation from Willard and subsequent adjustment to being a single mom was one of the most difficult periods of my life. I thanked God for Eva who listened and encouraged me every step of the way.

One of the first things that happened to me was a shocking rebuke from the pastor of our church. He called me into his office and told me that because I left my husband, God would put me on a shelf and never use me again. Devastated and deeply hurt, I ran from the church, humiliated and defeated. I was filled with guilt and begged God for mercy.

Because I had so many demands on me, however, I had little time to dwell on what the pastor had said. I kept going to work, encouraging Kevan and attending to my daughter.

I began enjoying my new home and worked at making it a loving place for Kevan and Keely. It was such a spirit of freedom not to have to walk on eggshells to please Willard, but I still had moments of self-doubt. I was filled with mixed emotions.

Coupled with the spiritual and emotional struggles, finances became a huge problem. My small salary at the nursing home barely covered the cost of my rent. I knew I had to look for a better job. A friend told me that Philco Ford was hiring and if I could get a job there, I would make twice what I was making at the nursing home. I began praying. With the exception of a small factory job I held years earlier, the nursing home was the only job I had ever had. So the prospect of working in a big place like Philco Ford was frightening. Nevertheless, I put in my application and in a few days I had a job. God answered my prayer.

The job they assigned me challenged my will, my body and my mind. Every night I came home discouraged and was sure I would never be able to do it. It was tedious work, and I had to manipulate tiny parts that I kept dropping. I felt like I was all thumbs. I prayed all day on the job and cried all night. Finally, one day it just happened. I could do it!

I began attending a small Southern Baptist church where I found a family of believers who loved and accepted me. Their patient encouragement brought immense healing to a woman who had been broken to bits. When my friend, Hedy, came for a visit and confirmed with loving assurance that God loved me and would again use me, I began feeling peace creep into my heart.

I fixed an area in my apartment so that I could again take a few reflexology appointments to supplement my income. Soon several of my clients I had been working on before I left Willard began coming regularly.

At the sign shop where Kevan worked, he met a fellow named Pete, and they soon became good friends. Before long they began discussing the idea of opening their own sign shop in Pete's barn. If Kevan could come up with $1000 for his part in the venture, they felt they could swing it. When Kevan reluctantly asked if I could lend the money to him, I was happy to do it. I know it was God's plan because I would not normally have had that much money I could give him. Thus began KAP Brothers Signs and I was the proudest mother alive.

Kevan tried to keep his father in his life, but Willard showed little interest. He longed for his dad's approval, but he always came home discouraged and disappointed after visiting him.

After I had been at Philco Ford for 6 months, I was laid off. The next day, I was standing in line at the unemployment office applying for benefits. While laid off, I began taking more reflexology clients and together with my unemployment, I squeaked by.

Hard at work at Philco Ford

Chapter Thirty-two

Graduation

While Keely was a resident at Ridge Crest, she was transported to a school near Doylestown, Pennsylvania. She continued attending there until she was twenty-one at which time she was no longer eligible for public education. At her graduation ceremony, she sat with her classmates, smiling and gently rocking back and forth in her cap and gown. I dabbed at the tears escaping my eyes. Her cap had slipped to one side and the teacher repositioned it as she handed Keely her diploma.

My mind drifted back to the day I placed Keely in the Wrens Preschool program 19 years earlier. I had such high hopes for her. I knew her life would never be normal, but I really thought she could be trained to speak, to handle some personal care, learn socially appropriate behavior and other skills that would improve her life. Yet, despite years of programs, Keely's behavior had changed very little. Her biggest change had come in the area of socialization. She knew how to sit quietly if she felt good. Also, she greeted people with a smile and was comfortable in social situations.

The moment Keely's hand grasped her diploma, she giggled and crumpled it excitedly.

Keely did not completely adjust to life in Ridge Crest. She had good days and bad, but every time I took her back after weekend visits, she would cry and bite her finger. I don't know if it was the hyperactivity of some of the other children in the program, whether it was the fact that she missed her brother and me, or the long bus ride to school every day that upset her. Possibly, it was all these and some I wasn't even aware of. I wanted to bring her home, but was not sure what to do. What if Philco called me back to work? If they did, then I wouldn't be able to keep Keely at home. What if they didn't call me back and my unemployment ran out? I would have to get another job. Life was certainly a challenge. However, as it turned out, I didn't have to make that decision. The administrative office called and asked me to come in to discuss Keely. During the meeting, I was told that Keely was not adjusting to life at Ridge Crest and perhaps I should look into a group home setting for her.

"I will take her home. I do not want her in a group home," I said.

"Not so fast, Claudette. We have to go through the discharge process and discuss the best options for Keely first."

A few weeks later they called me with a date and time for the meeting, and I went alone. Several professionals were present to give their input, and they all leaned toward me placing Keely in a group home.

They thought that it would be too difficult to have Keely at home since I was now a single working mom.

I felt like I was on trial and defenseless. Elyse Fox spoke up and said she would like to suggest that Claudette be free to take Keely home in her care.

"I know Claudette very well, and she is quite capable of caring for her daughter." At that everyone stood and agreed. Elyse put her arms around me, and I cried and thanked her. I will always be grateful for her.

I went to the office, signed papers, packed Keely's things and brought her home. She had been at Ridge Crest about a year.

Chapter Thirty-three

Reconciliation?

I had been separated from Willard for two years
when a friend told me about a Christian conference in
Philadelphia led by Bill Gothard. I signed up to go and
persuaded Kevan to go with me. It was at this
conference where I learned how my troubled childhood
had affected my life.

First, losing my mother at age 4 interrupted a
very important relationship in my life—the mother-
daughter bond that began in the womb of my mother.

During the preschool years I was cuddled,
encouraged and cherished. I clung to Mommy when
frightened, hurt or confused. I loved the fairy tales she
read to me and I pictured myself as a princess. My
beautiful mother brushed my hair, tucked me into bed
each night, played with me and conveyed unconditional

love. Did these things happen? Probably, but sadly I have no memory of them.

In spite of having love and care from my Grammy and Aunt Margaret following my mother's death, they were not Mother. They couldn't replace her, even though they tried.

Throughout my life, even today, I have moments when I wonder about my mother. What was she like? Was she a warm person? Outgoing? Shy? Musical? Artistic? Family members who knew her gave me bits of information, but my father would not talk to me about her. No matter how hard I tried, I couldn't piece together a clear image of her. She was like a phantom in my life, a shadow.

A mother is a teacher, a role model, and an encourager. Growing up with a step-mother who was not able to be those things to me left a huge hole in my emotional make-up. I especially needed encouragement. I needed to know I was "okay," and that I wasn't ugly or stupid. Dropping out of school compounded these feelings of inferiority.

So what does all this have to do with the direction of my life? I was drawn to people who I thought demonstrated those qualities of a mother—

Carolyn Bergey, Betty Barndt, Eva Bosh, Cindy Longacre, Marion Moser, Lola Huntsinger, Betty Mussleman and more. The list was endless! I was driven to learn from them, to be encouraged by them and to prove to myself I was a worthy person. This, then, is what I call the search for my mother. Consequently, I spent time with friends, learning and growing from them whenever my schedule allowed. This contributed to Willard's chosen label for me—a run-around. My search for emotional fulfillment took me outside my marriage and it damaged it.

Secondly, when Daddy married Beulah, I felt abandoned. Yes, he provided for my physical needs, but I no longer felt safe. I was at the mercy of Beulah. Why did he allow me to be treated the way I was? Because he did not step up and protect me and be my advocate, I believe I lost respect for him. My love for him never changed and I forgave him years ago, but deep down, I was angry with him and did not look up to him as I once did. Subconsciously, shortly after the birth of Keely, I transferred that lack of respect to my husband. How could I look up to a man who wouldn't undergird me with his support? Obviously, couples who lack repect for each other will inevitably damage their marriage relationship.

Thirdly, for as long as I can remember, I have felt an intense desire to relieve the suffering of others. My heart was touched when I saw injustice and pain even as a child. As an adult that empathy was extended to causes for the retarded, the Vietnamese family, Fresh Air kids and many, many more. All during Keely's life, I did my best to keep her as pain free as possible. My desire to help others seemed to know no bounds.

The result was that I became involved in many situations that took me out of the home and kept me on the phone for hours. Of course, this distressed Willard and served to further damage our relationship.

I had become a strong-willed and independent woman. The result was that I felt "qualified" to change my husband. Needless to say, my spirit of independence and self-righteousness eroded my marriage.

I am certainly not saying my marriage failed because of me alone. My frustration with Willard has been made clear throughout this book. I am not responsible for Willard's role in our marriage, but for my own.

God used the Gothard seminar to help me see an important truth. As a Christian, no matter how troubled my childhood was, or how unhappy, tired or frustrated I was, I transgressed God's law when I left Willard. I came away convicted that I had done a terrible thing by walking out on my marriage, and I should try and make amends. I hoped it wasn't too late.

I wrote a letter to Willard and asked him if we could meet and talk.

He called shortly after getting the letter.

"Claudie, I got your letter," he said. His voice revealed his nervousness.

"Willard, I was wrong to leave you. I want you to know that I'm sorry."

"What are you going to do?" he asked.

"Well, I'm not getting an attorney or suing you for a divorce."

There was no response for several moments.

"What about the house?" he asked, finally. It was then I knew that Willard had no intention of meeting to "talk."

"Willard, I don't care about the house." We hung up on that note. Why did I think Willard and I could talk? For twenty-three years, we couldn't talk. A few days later he called to ask me if I was serious about not wanting the house.

"Yes, I was serious, Willard."

I had no fight left in me. Whatever Willard wanted to do was fine. I only wanted to do what I felt God wanted me to do.

In a few months I signed divorce papers and accepted the small settlement that Willard offered me. Willard remarried sometime thereafter.

I knew that God had forgiven me for what I had done and I had peace in my heart.

My twin Polly and me

Chapter Thirty-four

A Group Home

Kevan came home from work one day and told me about a house for rent he and Pete had seen while they were doing some sign work in Perkasie.

"It's a really big house, Mom, and the rent is only $275 a month."

"Are you sure, Kevan?" I asked. My apartment rent was much more than that so I couldn't imagine a whole house would cost so little.

"It's probably a dump," I said.

"No, it's not. It looks really nice, at least on the outside. I was thinking you and Eva could rent it together. You could split the rent and have plenty of room for a reflexology office."

Kevan was so excited and it rubbed off on me. I called Eva and we made an appointment to go see the house. It was on Market Street, and it was huge! I counted three bedrooms on the third floor and five on the second floor. On the first floor was a living room, dining room and a kitchen. An insurance office occupied three rooms on one side, but the rest of the house would easily accommodate both families. And it wasn't a dump!

We walked around trying to imagine how best to divide the house so that we could have separate living areas. But could two women share the same house? Eva and I were completely different. I was outgoing and loved lots of company. Eva, on the other hand, was quiet and preferred a subdued lifestyle. Although we had already shared an apartment for a short time when I left Willard, we were somewhat reluctant at the thought of living under the same roof permanently.

However, we kept coming back to the thought that we would only have to pay $137.50 each. What a huge help that would be for both of us. Our kids could live in a house with a yard once again! We could not pass up the opportunity. That evening we signed the papers and returned to our separate apartments to plan our move.

I secured a part-time job with Dr. Thomas Marsteller, a naturopathic doctor in Sellersville, and I set up an office in our new home to continue my reflexology practice. It was a busy time, full of adjustments. We rearranged the house numerous times to make it fit our lifestyles. I had an office upstairs, then downstairs. I had a makeshift kitchen upstairs and then scrapped that idea. Eva had a living room upstairs, then downstairs. She had a bedroom on the third floor, then on the second floor. In spite of the size of the house, it had only one bathroom and only one kitchen. Those were the biggest problems. Eventually, we gave up trying to keep totally separate quarters and faced reality. We simply made it a home for a diversified family—a kind of "group home."

After Keely finished her schooling at age twenty-one, she attended the daycare center for learning disabled located near Ridge Crest. Her petit mal seizures seemed to worsen and then one afternoon she had a grand mal seizure. I had seen other children seizure, but seeing my own child go through that was devastating. *What else, Lord?*

I called her doctor and he prescribed Phenobarbital. Overnight Keely began having anger outbursts and lashing out at others. It was shocking to see for it was not at all like the Keely we knew. When she would have one of these events, she would cry and scream at the top of her lungs and shake her hands in rage. I'm sure it sounded like she was being beaten to anyone listening. Once a neighbor who heard her screams actually called the police and an officer knocked on the front door to investigate. He was apologetic when he learned the problem.

I had always been able to take Keely to church or out for a burger, but it became a big problem to take her anywhere. I never knew what would set her off. I don't know how many times I had to get up and take her out of church in the middle of an outburst.

For a time, I blamed myself thinking that I had disrupted her life again by bringing her home. However as the months passed, I began suspecting her temper tantrums were related to the Phenobarbital because it was after she started on it that her behavior changed. I called her doctor and pleaded with him to try another medication for the seizures. He put her on Dilantin which controlled the seizures and returned Keely to the sweet girl we all knew.

Willard had begun taking Keely on occasional

Saturday afternoons during this period in her life. He would pick her up and take her to his mother's home in Souderton. Mrs. Price loved Keely deeply and when she died the relationship between Keely and Willard died as well because he ceased all visits with his daughter.

Keely received a check each month from Social Security, but that did not begin to cover all her expenses. Her medications, clothing and disposable diapers alone ate up most of the check. Every day I had mountains of laundry because Keely drooled and soiled her clothes daily and wet the bed every night. I had to have help. Willard was her father and our divorce did not change that fact. I went to see my attorney who filed for child support.

The attorney spoke calmly, but firmly as he reminded Willard that he had a dependent daughter who needed his help. In the end, Willard was required to pay child support. After that meeting, all communication ceased between Willard and me, not that there ever had been *real* communication.

Several months later Kevan got a call from his dad's brother letting him know Willard had had bypass surgery. When Kevan went to see his dad, once again he came home with hurt feelings. I knew if Willard didn't try to relate to Kevan soon, it would be too late.

Keely and Kevan

Keely and Sherry (Eva's daughter)

Sherry and my niece, Amy

217

My niece, Tamara, and Sherry

Kevan

218

Chapter Thirty-five

Personal Growth

Music had always played an important role in my life as well as Keely's. When she was upset about something, I could usually calm her by cranking up the radio or popping in one of her gospel music tapes. I had been singing all my life. I sang in the car, at church, while doing housework and while tending to Keely. Actually, Keely was my best audience, rocking in rhythm to whatever song I sang. She often "sang" along, perfect in pitch and tune, but unable to vocalize. I longed to take voice lessons, but never had the opportunity to pursue that dream. A friend at church was taking voice lessons, and she encouraged me to follow my dream. I called a local music director, Joanne Lupino, who agreed to take me on as a student. I flew home excited to share the news with Eva.

Taking lessons proved to be one of the best decisions I had ever made. Little did I know then how God would use my music in the years that followed to bless my heart, lighten Keely's moods, minister to my church family and later in a nursing home ministry.

The job I had taken with Dr. Marsteller had opened the whole world of holistic medicine to me. I learned much about healing herbs, chiropractic medicine and other natural healing modalities. At the same time, my own reflexology business was growing, and I began thinking about leaving the doctor's office and doing reflexology full time. It was a big step of faith knowing I would need a steady income. I did take the step and God proved faithful.

True to Hedy's affirmation, God did not put me on a shelf, but began using me in my local church. My involvement with parent groups and other organizations that had consumed me during Keely's early years had changed dramatically, and I began devoting more time to my church. At various times, I served as a Sunday school teacher, director of our mission organization, Vacation Bible School worker, a committee member and even as a choir director for a while. In my *spare* time, I often mowed the grass at church, painted and cleaned. Usually I took Keely with me. She would rock and listen to music as I worked.

I loved my church and every pastor ministered to Keely and me in a special way. Former pastors, John MacIntyre, John Hackworth, and Mark Dooley were all so kind and understanding with Keely and me. I will be eternally grateful for their visits, encouragement and prayers. My pastor today, Justin Glenn, has likewise shown great compassion and I feel blessed once again.

I learned early on that I could not out-give God. The more I gave to others and to my church, the more I was blessed in return. Sometimes Kevan would admonish me by saying I was giving too much. He knew he would always get a sermon from me on giving if he tried to influence me in that area.

I found my reflexology business had become a source of counseling. During treatments, my clients relaxed, trusted me and often confided their concerns to me. I was able to share God's Word with many of them, pray with them and introduce them to the Life-giver. In turn, my clients became my friends and my greatest support system. They prayed for me, brought Keely and me gifts on our birthdays and Christmas, and were eager to help me during difficult times. After their treatment, many clients would spend a few minutes talking with Keely and would drop off a stuffed animal for her. A client returned from vacation one day and brought me a dish in the shape of a foot. That began my foot collection. From then on, clients brought me all kinds of feet for my collection. It added to the uniqueness of my office. I cannot begin to say enough about the satisfaction, joy and love I have because of clients. There simply are no appropriate words.

Chapter Thirty-six

Family Life

Eva's children were growing up. Her oldest daughter had gone away to college and her oldest son into the service. We spent a lot of time together discussing issues and hoping we were providing the best possible home for our children. It was certainly never dull. We always had something going on. It might be a birthday party, a Christmas party or just a party. Keely delighted in all the festivities. She would rock back and forth, giggling to herself.

The kids welcomed their friends over and the neighbors felt free to drop in for coffee and a chat. We had many fun times as our two families practically merged into one. Our children loved each other and got along fine together. Eva often sat with Keely when I was working, and I sat with her youngest two while she worked. We made a good team even if we weren't the typical family.

Nevertheless, from time to time we discussed the idea of going our separate ways. However, our lives had become so intertwined, it was frightening to think of trying to make it alone. We were definitely better off financially by staying together, and we depended on each other for child care. We had functioned as one family, so I suppose we felt as though it would be like going through another divorce.

The question came up seriously, however, when Jack Maddox, a man who attended our church, called Eva for a date in 1979. I knew they liked each other, but I was not ready to face life alone again. *How will I handle Keely? Where will I live?* I grew to resent Jack. I'm sure he knew that. I liked the life we had, and I wanted to hang on to it.

Eva's youngest son was going through a rebellious time in his teen years, and it was a huge worry to her. She was scared she would lose him. Her concern for her son and her own insecurities prompted her to back away from Jack. Her divorce had only been over a few months, and she felt she simply wasn't ready for a serious relationship.

Soon after that our landlord called to say he was selling the house. It seemed like I always had some big hurdle to jump over. Now what? I had no money. Eva had no money. It took every penny she and I could scrape together just to exist. Once again, we thought about getting separate apartments. And once again, we didn't think we could. God would have to provide because we couldn't imagine what we were going to do.

I was driving home from work one day and noticed a big sign, "House for rent." It was hanging on the porch rail of a house in Sellersville. Even though I had doubts that we could afford it, or worse yet, rent it to two women and four children, nevertheless, I pulled over, scribbled down the telephone number and hurried home to call. Again, God answered prayer. Not only would the man rent it to us, the rent was within our range, and they offered us a three-year option to buy!

It was a lovely old Victorian house with lots of room. The third floor had two bedrooms and the second had four. It even had an extra bathroom! I would have a spacious office and a waiting room. God is good. We moved into our new home in the early spring of 1983.

Eva and me at our church's Harvest Gathering

Our house on Walnut Street

Chapter Thirty-seven

Changes, Changes . . .

Keely enjoyed a relatively healthy period of time in spite of her chronic problems. She could walk with assistance and speak a few words and loved to listen to the radio with her earphones. Going for rides and chomping on a cheeseburger were two of her favorite things.

When Kevan would occasionally ask Keely if she wanted to go for a ride in his truck, she would giggle and say "truck" and hop up ready to go. It was always a special treat for Keely to spend time with her brother.

Kevan met and married Alisha Albright, a

wonderful girl who attended our church. Alisha was beautiful, but more importantly, she was a Christian. I was so happy and proud of both of them. Fortunately, they settled nearby and remained loyal and supportive

to Keely and to me. Kevan had invited his father to his wedding, but Willard did not attend. I felt sorry for Kevan.

I had remained in contact with several parents of retarded children in the area, and knew the sorrow, distress and loneliness they all experienced as they dealt with their special children day after day. Once again, I saw the need to start a parent group. We all needed someone who could really understand our concerns and anguish.

I telephoned a number of parents and told them my idea to start a group again, and they were happy to participate. We met around the dining room table at our home and decided to call ourselves SPARC (Supportive Parents Association for Retarded Children). SPARC continued for several years and served its purpose. We were able to cry together, discuss issues that came up in the daycare program and encourage one another.

I had begun to hope that Keely's health was going to remain stable when she suddenly began crying and running a temperature. She was later diagnosed with mononucleosis. She was so sick I actually thought she was going to die. Whenever Keely caught something, she was always much sicker than the average person. Her immune system was compromised, and she was unable to throw off illnesses very fast. Weeks went by and little by little Keely improved and regained her strength.

Each time she went through a serious illness, I was stressed to the limit as I cared for her and still continued to see clients. Only through the strength God gave me was I able to do it.

In 1986 our three-year agreement for an option to buy our house was nearing the deadline. Neither Eva nor I had been able to save a down payment. Eva had a job that barely covered her financial needs and despite the fact that my business was doing well, I was barely making it. We were at a loss as to what our next move would be. I put in a call to my sister, Gail, who I thought might consider loaning us the down payment. I knew Gail had been successful in investing and probably had the means to do it. It was not easy to make that call. I was nervous, but I knew I had to push past my feelings. It seemed like I had been doing that all my life anyway, so one more time wouldn't matter I told myself.

Gail agreed to loan us the money and drew up a mortgage plan for us to repay the loan. We signed the papers and Eva and I became co-homeowners.

Eva's youngest son graduated from high school and joined the army, and her youngest daughter finished school and moved into her own apartment. That left Eva, Keely and me for a short time in the house. It wasn't long, though, before her oldest daughter divorced and came home with a baby boy to stay with us for about a year. Following that, her youngest son returned after his stint overseas and lived with us also for a time. It seems we were always having either one of the kids coming home, or we were taking in someone else who needed a home.

My friend, Joan, desperately needed to escape from a relationship, and Eva and I agreed to let her stay with us for two months until she found a place of her own. Another friend, Dawn, had left an abusive relationship, and we took her in until she married.

There were many words that could describe our life on Walnut Street in Sellersville. Interesting, fun, stressful, and happy – are a few that come to mind.

After all the children seemed to be settled in their lives, Eva, Keely and I were the only ones left in the house. After all the activity we had grown used to, the house seemed big and empty. We began looking around for a smaller place. I had taken Keely out for a drive one day when I spotted a small rancher on Lawn Avenue near the hospital. I took down the telephone number and hurried home to call.

The house was certainly different from any we had ever seen. It had three small bedrooms and a full bathroom downstairs in the basement. The main floor featured a nice size living room with a fireplace, a kitchen, dining area and another bath. The best feature of the property was that it had a separate building on it that could be made into an office for me. It would be wonderful not to have clients coming in and out of the house. In addition the house was a stone's throw from the hospital and Keely's daycare. It seemed perfect for us. If only we had enough equity in our house to handle the down payment.

When we made application, we were surprised

to discover that the market had grown to the point that the value of our house had almost doubled! We thanked God for his provision for us and we moved into the Lawn Avenue house in 1986.

Chapter Thirty-eight

Blessings and Disappointments

Kevan and Alisha had their first child, a little girl they named Julie Alston. Immediately, I understood bragging grandmothers. I was so proud and delighted of that little bundle and so relieved to see she was perfect.

Although I had not voiced it, I had been fearful that Keely's syndrome would be genetic, even though the doctor had assured me it wasn't.

A few years prior, Kevan and Pete had decided to dissolve their business and Kevan went to work for another sign company. He worked there until he started his own shop that he called Horizon Signs.

"I want to be available to help you, Mom, if a problem arises, and I can do that if I have my own shop." His words touched my heart and again I thanked God for such a caring son.

Kevan and Alisha settled into a home minutes from me and were so willing to pitch in and help me every time they could. It was such a comfort having them nearby. I decided, however, I would not be a meddling mother-in-law. I didn't have time to do that anyway. Between Keely, my home, the church and my business, I was a very busy woman.

Kevan and Alisa had two more children in the next few years. Chelsea Benner and Keely Ann. Benner was my mother's maiden name and my middle name. Keely Ann, of course, was named after my Keely. The fact that they would name the baby "Keely" shocked me and brought tears to my eyes. It was one of the nicest things anyone had ever done for me.

I loved all three of my grandchildren. I tried to be an involved grandmother as much as possible with my limited time. I alternated having each of them over on Friday nights, taking them to dinner and watching videos with them.

Small children were frequently scared of Keely, realizing there was something different about her. However, from the time my granddaughters were babies, they had no fear of Keely. They hugged and kissed her and showered her with love and affection. Their acceptance and love of Keely means more to mean than I can ever express. Keely loves them as well. She would shake her head and laugh whenever she heard their voices.

In spite of all my responsibilities, I managed to maintain some of my personal interests. I loved southern gospel music and attended a few concerts with a friend whenever I was able to arrange a sitter for Keely. In addition, I began a nursing home ministry, going to four nursing homes on a monthly rotating basis, singing songs, telling jokes and encouraging the patients. Often I would take one of my grandchildren or the pastor's children with me. The older folks in the homes loved the children and genuinely appreciated us coming.

Besides the nursing homes, I was asked to sing

at a number of special events through the years and even made a CD of my favorite songs. Many have told me they were blessed by the songs I recorded.

With all of Eva's children on their own, she began seeing Jack Maddox again. They dated most of 1990 and were married in September of that year. It was a difficult time for me once again. We had lived as one family for eleven years, and I felt abandoned and scared. I was so used to discussing everything with Eva and relying on her in so many ways, and that changed dramatically when she married.

A Christian man who had been attending our church called and asked if I would go to dinner with him and I agreed. He was good-looking, fun to be with and he related well with Keely. He was a charming man who came into my life at a critical moment. I believed him when he said he loved me and we married in 1991.

Life with Walt was troubling almost from the first day. We could not communicate and I was at the end of my rope. *How did I allow myself to get into this predicament?* It was another painful time in my life. I went away for a weekend with Jack and Eva, leaving a note for Walt. The words were painful to write, but my only recourse. I told him to pack his bags and leave the house by the time I returned home if he had no intention of working on our relationship. When I returned, he was gone. Our marriage lasted seven months.

I don't know what happened between us, but I know we had loved each other. I also know divorce is wrong. However, in order to have the strength to care for my daughter, I had to have emotional peace of mind. I couldn't live in a state of frustration, worry and panic. Keely had to be first in my life. Perhaps that is the answer to what happened.

Some residents in one of the nursing homes I visit monthly. I'm in the back row left with granddaughters, Chelsea and Keely on right.

Keely gets a reflexology treatment

Chapter Thirty-nine

Coping with Illness

After Walt and I divorced, I decided to move our bedrooms upstairs to the living room because it had become increasingly difficult for Keely to climb steps. It cut down on our living space, but I did the best I could to make it as homey as possible.

With three empty bedrooms, I hoped to rent the rooms out in order to subsidize my income. It didn't take long to do that. I rented the rooms to a number of people in the next few years and gradually updated the area to create a small apartment. It was comforting to know someone else was nearby if I needed help.

After graduating from public school, Keely went directly into daycare. It was a huge help to me because I could work during the hours she was there and didn't have to pay a babysitter. The daycare she attended was one of the services that grew out of Ridge Crest. Although Keely had been in many different programs since she was two years old, she never completely fit in any one program. Either she was higher functioning, lower functioning or socially didn't fit. The current daycare was no different.

There were several clients who were hyperactive, jumping around the room and bumping into Keely. She came home with bruises and scratches and several incident reports were filed. She was obviously disturbed by the noise and confusion of the room and many times when I went to pick her up, I would find her either crying or alone in a room. In addition, since she did not handle change well, each time there was a staff change, she would be confused and irritable.

During the next few years, I had a number of surgical interventions myself that required extra caregivers for Keely. I had a hysterectomy, hiatal hernia surgery, carpal tunnel surgery on both hands and an inguinal hernia. These were difficult times for Keely since routine was critical for her emotional stability. I had so many friends who stood by me, encouraging me and praying for me. I thank God for them even as I write these words. It was amazing how God took care of my financial needs through friends and family members. Bill and Carol Beeman were so supportive of me and were willing to help any way they could. They had a foster son for a time who had learning disabilities, and they truly understood what it was like to care for a child like Keely.

Bill and Carol Beeman

From time to time my church tried implementing a schedule of helpers to come and sit with Keely so that I could attend church. It would work for a while, but Keely's health was unpredictable.

Therefore, each time a new schedule was arranged Keely would end up sick or in the hospital and the schedule abandoned. I am grateful, though, for all the support they have given me through the years.

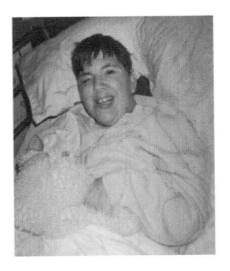

Keely's beautiful smile

Chapter Forty

Growing Weaker

By the time Keely had reached age thirty, her daily personal care routine took almost two hours every morning. She woke, usually with a wet bed, and although she weighed about 150 pounds, I was still able to manage giving her a tub bath. Keely tried so hard to cooperate with whatever I was doing. When her bath was finished I would say, "Hold Mommy's arm, Keely," and she would wrap her arm around mine. It was not easy getting her out of the tub, and a few times she slipped from my arm and fell back into the water.

Keely had poor muscle tone and could not easily form her stools often requiring an enema or suppositories to help her eliminate. Sometimes it meant leaving her on the potty for 10-15 minutes, while all the time I felt pressured so I could be ready for my first client. Patience is one thing Keely has taught me. I could never hurry her. I could only slow me down.

Since Keely could do none of her own personal care, I had to brush her teeth, dress her and comb her hair. She always had a variety of medications to take and eye salve to apply. Once all that was done, I prepared breakfast, fed her and put her bedclothes in the laundry. I usually had about ten minutes to get dressed for work.

From the time Keely was 38 years old, her health continued to spiral downward. In the mid 1990's she began walking with great difficulty and crying as though in pain. The doctor ordered x-rays, and the films revealed that she had bone deformities in her hips and neck as well as scoliosis of the spine. However, he did not think that was the cause of her pain. Her crying continued for months.

Keely began refusing food, crying and biting her finger. Tests revealed she had a non-functioning gall bladder, and she was admitted to Grand View Hospital for surgery. Almost immediately she was pain free.

It was about this time that a social worker, Heather Davis, from Penn Foundation entered our lives. Heather helped me with doctor visits, paper work and a

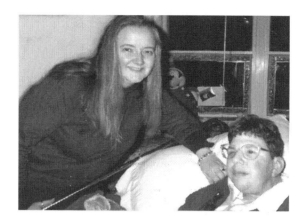

Heather and Keely

host of other concerns. She became much more than a social worker; she became a friend and an advocate. I thanked God many times for Heather who remains a vital part of our lives even today.

When Keely was about forty she began refusing food again, losing weight, crying and biting her finger. As I was bathing her one morning, I heard an odd rumbling in her chest and immediately called Dr. Rousche. Tests revealed Keely had a large hiatal hernia. I dreaded thinking about Keely having more surgery, but she couldn't live with the pain she had been having for months. I was at my wits end with all the crying.

At the daycare, the workers appeared not to take Keely's health issues seriously even though I continually explained that something was really wrong with her physically. I could no longer deal with the situation at the daycare center, and I told Heather I was taking her out of the program. Heather made arrangements with the director, Sharon Young, for Keely to be dismissed from the program. Sharon agreed that the best thing for Keely would be home care with financial assistance provided by the county. Darlene Hamburger, my neighbor, was hired by KenCrest to be Keely's caregiver. She faithfully cared for her for several years until Keely's health warranted more specialized help.

Keely began vomiting and gagging, and Dr. Rousche insisted that Keely needed surgery and referred her to Dr. Rilling. He operated on her and Keely spent the next six weeks in the hospital.

Every time Keely was hospitalized, I stayed with her day and night, watching over her, assisting the nurses and making sure Keely knew I was there. Heather, of course, went with me and was like a rock I could lean on. The doctors and nurses and aides grew to know and love Keely and often dropped in to say hello. Family and friends always called and stopped by as well, and the church helped me with a gift of money.

I was unable to work when Keely was hospitalized and, consequently, the loss of income was a huge problem. However, I had no recourse but to focus on my daughter and trust God to see me through. I was determined not to rely on my son, but he was quick to loan me what he could, and I always managed to repay him. God provided for me in miraculous ways through unexpected gifts from friends who understood my situation.

I had become acquainted with Shirley Thomas some years earlier and eventually trained and certified her in reflexology. Shirley became one of my dearest friends. We had an agreement during times of Keely's setbacks that she would use my office and treat my clients and we would share the income. That was a big help.

About a year later, Keely again began crying and wincing in pain. I pleaded with Dr. Rousche to have x-rays taken because I knew something was wrong. I had cared for Keely so long that I could sense when something was not right. This was one of those times.

Dr. Rousche ordered x-rays but nothing showed on the films. Keely was okay according to the gastroenterologist. I knew Keely was far from okay because she would lie quietly in bed for a few moments and then scream in pain, biting down hard on her finger. She alternated day and night between quiet moments and screaming.

Finally, in desperation, I took out my video camera and captured what I had been trying to tell the doctors. Once they saw for themselves, they knew Keely had a serious problem. They determined that the incision from her hiatal hernia surgery had opened. She was operated on again and a mesh placed in the incision to prevent further herniation.

Dr. Rousche gets a smooch

Chapter Forty-one

Fifty Years!

By this time I could no longer manage Keely's tub baths and asked my brother, John, to remodel my bathroom and install a walk-in shower. I obtained a hospital bed and a wheelchair for Keely which made caring and transporting her much easier.

Two years later, Keely began having the same symptoms she had prior to her hiatal hernia surgery and when tested, they found the  hiatal hernia was back. Dr. Rilling operated on her again. Keely had had so many surgeries that she was full of scar tissue. The doctor advised that any further surgery for Keely would be far too risky.

A year later, I woke one morning to find Keely wedged in the rails of her bed, barely alive. She had suffered a grand mal seizure during the night, and I had not heard a thing. I thought my heart was going to stop as I phoned Kevan.

Kevan carried Keely to the shower and I massaged her with warm water trying to get a response out of her. When she revived a bit, Kevan carried her to the recliner, and I wrapped her in a warm blanket and called the doctor. She was bruised in several places, but x-rays revealed no broken bones. A second medication was added to the dilantin to control her seizures.

It was during this time that I began feeling the support of the medical community—Drs. Rilling, Kucer and especially Rousche. Dr. Rousche had become more than a physician to us, she had become our friend. No matter how many times I've had to call her, she has never been impatient or frustrated with me. When I have any concern about something Keely is experiencing, she listens to me and follows through with treatment. What a privilege and a blessing!

As Keely's condition worsened, she reached a point where she was no longer unable to walk. Therefore, I had to transport her with a wheelchair. In order to do this, I had to have a way to get her in and out of the house. Kevan agreed to build a deck with a ramp on the back of the house, and I put in a driveway.

There was always a huge expense each time an adjustment had to be made to accommodate Keely's needs. Coupled with all the expenses of daily living, I was forced to refinance my house several times. I hated doing that, but had no choice. Kevan and Alisha invited Keely and me to come and live with them, but I did not want to burden them.

When Keely was about 45 years old, she began having choking episodes and recurring bouts of pneumonia. It was terrifying to watch my child gasp for breath. The doctor ordered a suction machine, and we suctioned her frequently to clear her air passage. She continued to worsen until it was obvious something else had to be done for her. She was hospitalized again. Her hiatal hernia had returned for the third time. She wouldn't eat or drink and the doctors said I had a big decision to make. The only way to save Keely's life was to put her on a feeding tube. *Should I let Keely starve to death? Did she have any real life left in her? Would it be more humane just to let her go?* I cried out to God to give me wisdom to make the right decision.

I looked into this child's face and saw what nobody else saw. It was the little girl that God entrusted me with forty-five years ago. I saw her innocence and the trust in her eyes as she looked back at me. I couldn't let her go. I just couldn't do it. Right or wrong, I made my decision. I know that many disagreed with it, but perhaps if she had been their child, they would have understood. It didn't really matter, though, if they understood or not. What mattered to me was Keely.

The feeding tube was put in and Keely returned home in about six weeks only to return a year later when the site became infected. The doctor removed that tube and inserted another one in a second site.

Keely's feeding tube had to be changed frequently which meant a trip to the hospital each time. And although it became increasingly difficult to hoist her into the wheelchair and down the ramp to my van, I was still able to manage it.

In spite of all that Keely went through, when she had pain relief, she was a happy girl who loved her mom, her music and her caregivers.

Keely's last surgery (at least the last I'll write about) was an insertion of a cecostomy tube. Once again, Keely began having severe pain and couldn't pass her stools. She choked and gagged and I was sick with worry. *They said no more surgery. Now what? I can't stand by and do nothing.* I took her to the hospital and pleaded with them to find out the cause of the pain. The doctor reminded me that any more surgery on Keely would be nearly impossible because of the scar tissue. Nevertheless, he did finally agree to do exploratory surgery. In doing so, he discovered a large obstruction in her bowel that had collected fecal matter and gas. He indicated that it had started two years ago when the gagging starting. He inserted a tube into Keely's bowel and she had almost immediate relief.

When Keely came home after the cecostomy surgery, her nursing care became overwhelming. Pat Martin, an employee from KenCrest came to visit and quickly determined that I needed more help than the caregivers currently working with Keely. She advised me that Keely needed an RN every day, and she would try to work toward that end. It took several weeks, but with Pat and Heather's help, I was approved. Keely would have the nursing care she needed.

Shortly after Keely had the cecostomy tube surgery, I began having trouble with my back. I attributed it to arthritis, but Dr. Rousche suggested an x-ray. By this time I felt like Grand View Hospital was my second home. The x-ray confirmed arthritis and to treat it with meds and rest. Dr. Rousche also said the x-ray report revealed "something" on the kidney and advised I have an MRI to determine what it was. When I got the news that I had a lesion, I was shocked, but hopeful it was nothing.

The surgeon said it could be cancer, but they wouldn't know that for sure until it was removed and a biopsy performed. Removal of the tumor, meant removal of my kidney. The news hit me like a ton of bricks. Cancer! Of course, I was devastated, but I began praying that I could accept whatever happened and trust it as God's will for me. The surgeon informed me that a rib would be removed to gain access to the kidney and that further added to my anxiety.

When my sister, Gail, and my other siblings heard that I was going to have a kidney removed, they rallied around me with love and support. I was especially grateful to them and despite the fact that we weren't involved in each other's day-to-day lives, we loved each other and that was so comforting to me.

Old friends that I hadn't heard from for a while called—Carolyn, Betty, Hedy, and Eva. What memories came with each call!

When the day of the surgery arrived, I had reached a point of accepting whatever happened. I just wanted it over, and I would deal with the consequences. In recovery, I was informed the surgeon had punctured my lung. Surprisingly, I had no drastic symptoms and remained in the hospital for several days recuperating, returning home on my 70th birthday.

When the news came that the tumor was cancerous, I was ready to hear it. God had given me strength to bear the devastating diagnosis.

Getting over the surgery and back to health was difficult for me. I had always been strong and full of energy, but now I lay unable to do anything but watch others care for Keely. I began thinking I should have taken my daughter-in-law's advice and gone home with them to recuperate. But little by little I regained my strength and in a few weeks, I was back to work. I would continue to have tests to see if the cancer appears anywhere else in my body. I thanked God for each new day.

The financial strain on me was often overwhelming although God had never let me down. Somehow things worked out in the strangest ways. One of these ways occurred one evening as I was sitting quietly having just changed into my pajamas when someone knocked softly on the front door. Standing there was a friend of mine, and she was holding something in her hand.

"Claudette, I won't stay because I know you're tired, but I want you to have this." She handed me a check.

When I saw the generous amount of the check, I did not want to take it, but she insisted. Tears formed in my eyes, and I gratefully accepted the gift that this angel unaware handed me. God had provided for me once again.

Keely is no longer able to get out of bed. Most

of the time, she is happy and contented. She will never be free of infections of one kind or another, and she will always need help. She will undoubtedly have more crises and when they happen, I lose all ability to focus on anything except her. That's why I have made preparations for her home-going to the great Life-Giver, Jesus, while I can think clearly. I have done the best I could possibly do for this child God gave me. I will stand before him with a clear conscious. There is peace in my heart.

I have not lived a perfect life. I made many mistakes on this journey of mine, but I know God understands and forgives me. I am eternally grateful.

I was humbled to be chosen for several awards during my lifetime and among them were the Lions Club Golden Deed Award and

the Courageous Parent of the Year Award from LifePath. No award in this life, however, will compare to the reward that I pray awaits me when the Lord greets me with, "Well done, good and faithful servant."

The night before Keely's 50th birthday, I clasped her small hands in mine and said, "Keely, tomorrow is your birthday!" She shook her head and laughed. Then I prayed with her as I had every night of her life.

On December 23, 2008, I watched Keely laughing with the guests at her 50th birthday party. Over fifty people came to the open house. There were doctors, nurses, caregivers, friends and family and it was the happiest day of Keely's life.

Keely's 50th Birthday Party

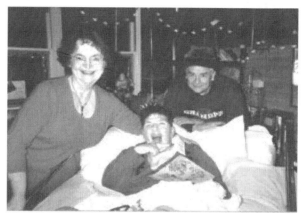

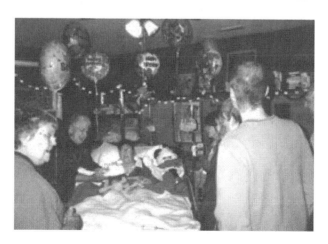

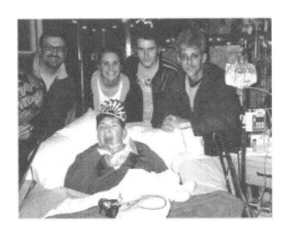

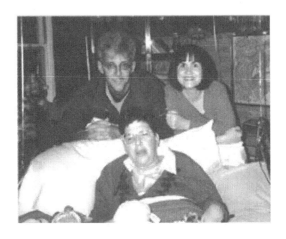

From Friends and Family . . .

Claudette and I have been devoted friends since 1976. We shared a home together for 11 years after we both experienced divorce. By combining incomes we were able to provide a house for our children to grow up in rather than cramped apartments.

"You never know a person until you live with them" is an old saying that I have found to be true. Claudie is the real deal. She's the same all decked out for a special event or padding around in her PJs. There's not a pretentious bone in her body.

We are two very different personalities. The noisier the house, the better she liked it. I preferred quiet. How many times have I said, "Could you just turn that down a notch?" Claudie was always hot natured, so she would turn the thermostat to 65. With teeth chattering, I would crank it up to 72. She liked company, I liked solitude. She was outgoing, and I more retiring. So how did we make it work for 11 years? I give her the credit. She is the one who made it work. She was the peacemaker.

Claudie is the hardest working person I have ever known. Whether it was working in the yard, cleaning house or painting a room, she kept at it until the job was done. Her only interruption was to stop and tend to Keely.

I cherish some memories of those years together. We could melt into laughter over absolutely nothing. Even as I write these words, I remember an incident that still elicits a smile. In was late evening and we were returning from a church event. Claudie was driving and I was in the passenger seat. She pulled up to the 5 points intersection traffic light in Sellersville. Out of the corner of my eye, I spied a burly, bearded man running toward the car. I screamed.

"Claudie, go!" She stepped on the gas, then realized the light was still red. So she jammed on the brakes.

"There's a man!" I shouted as he reached the car. Again she hit the gas, followed by the brake. (Excuse me, but I'm giggling as I try to write this!) While the car rocked back and forth, Claudie finally got the courage to roll down the window in time to hear the man shout disgustedly, "I just wanted to tell you your tail light was out!" At that, we got hysterical had to pull the car over until our laughing spasms slowed.

I miss our trips, our projects, our family get-togethers, my reflexology treatments and especially our hoagie nights!

Claudie has a heart for others. So many have been touched by her generosity, love and encouragement. She goes above and beyond what the average person does. She has shared her faith every time she was given the opportunity.

She has loved my children and taken them into her heart. Her devotion to Keely and Kevan is amazing. She is in love with her beautiful granddaughters. Her brothers and sister, nieces and nephews are very dear to her, and I know for a fact that she prays for all of them regularly. Her deep faith and trust in God is evident in everything she does.

I don't want to overlook the fact that Claudie can be a lot of fun! She can turn an event from boring to a blast in minutes.

I know I am blest by her friendship. What I would have missed had I not known her! I have a lot of friends and so does she, but only once in a lifetime do you get a Claudie.

Love to my dearest friend,
Eva Maddox

Through this book, I had the privilege of meeting Keely, Kevan and Claudette. *Keely, My Life-Changer,* is a remarkable story of love, devotion, and service. With her contagious smile, Keely captures the hearts of family, friends, and caregivers. She inspires her mother to go beyond her comfort zone,  enabling her to accomplish amazing things.
Wilma Caraway

My mom is the best! As a child, she made life seem normal even though I had a retarded sister. She was always able to fit in quality time when I needed it. As an adult, she has taught me to take life one day at a time. Her faith and hope in Christ makes her a beautiful person. Words cannot express what she means to me.
I love you, Mom
Kevan

 Claudette is an example of a faithful mother. She has sacrificed much in the way of personal freedom to care for Keely, but has done so willingly. In the 25 years that I have been in her family, I can honestly say that I have never heard her complain once about the tremendous amount of work that is involved with Keely's care. She depends on God to provide her with the strength she needs.
Love,
Alisha

Hey Gram! The main thing I think about when I think of my Aunt Keely is how she is always smiling. It doesn't matter if she's in a hospital bed or at home watching Sponge Bob! I remember sleeping over at your house and just watching her smile and laugh, bobbing her head as she listened to her country music and  watching us grandkids. She is a wonderful person to be around. She has taught me that no matter how bad things are, there is always a reason to smile.
Love you Aunt Kee and Gram!
Julie

 Ever since I was a little girl, I have looked up to my grandmother. Looking back at the 18 years we have spent together, I see what a blessing she has been to me. Life without Grammy is unthinkable! She is such a positive encouragement to me. She listens intently as I tell her all my crazy dreams, like being a lion tamer. "You can do anything you want if you work hard and put your mind to it," she would say. She has supported me 100%. As I see the impact she has had, not only on me, but on so many others, I pray that God will use me the same way. This summer she has trained and certified me in reflexology and I hope to bless others as she has blessed me. She has taught me so much about life and I thank God for her every day!
Love you Gram!
Chelsea Benner Price

4

My Grammy always made things so fun for me as a child. Going to Grammy's house on Friday night was a big deal. Aunt Keely was always there listening to her country music and nodding her head with a great big smile on  her face. Grammy is a very cheerful person to be around. I think that's great because I know that she doesn't have the easiest life. She just takes in one day at a time!

Love you Gram!
Keely Ann

 Keely and Claudette have been such an inspiration in my life. Claudette, for her dedication and perseverance. Keely, for her sweet personality. I don't see how anybody who could go through what they have without their strong faith in God. They also have a very close relationship with Kevan and his family which gives them a strong foundation.

From your loving sister and aunt,
Gail

I look back over your life and I wonder and hope that I could have made some of the decisions you have made. Your life has been a challenge. I have seen your ups and downs and I know only by the grace of God have you gotten through them. When I think back on your life and see where you have been, what you have accomplished, your pain, and also your times of joy, I am truly amazed and very proud of you. Keely's smile makes it all worthwhile, doesn't it?

Love forever,
Your brother, John

I have known Claudette and Keely for over 30 years and in those years I have, in part, developed my own identity by my relationship with them. Claudette

has been my care-giver, family, spiritual guide, encourager and friend. Keely has been an inspiration and a lesson in compassion. Some have said, "Why would God allow Keely and Claudette to struggle with mental and physical affliction?" They simply do not realize that Keely is truly a gift from God to Claudette. She is not a mistake or a handicap. Yes, Claudette has struggled with the challenges of life, but she knows that Keely is a beautiful child who has a purpose. It was Claudette's joy to discover it and share it with the world. I for one, am a better person having been a part of their lives.

Love,
Sherry Thompson (Eva's daughter)

Claudette and Keely have enriched my life by being flesh and blood examples of God's love. One of the most important lessons I have learned from their journey is that God doesn't always remove the storms of life, but he walks with us through them.
Betty J. Barndt

Without a doubt, what has impressed me most about Claudette is her steadfast faith in God in the face of adversity. I have learned much from her as I've watched her care for Keely for the past 40 years. Claudette trusts in God for all her needs and shamelessly shares her faith with others. I aspire to be a better Christian because of knowing her. She is a great friend and inspiration!
Cindy Longacre

Meeting and witnessing Claudette's faith in accepting her role as mother of Keely, a handicapped child, gives value to one's fate in life. She directed her energy to a more positive role, involving herself by always being ready to help and comfort others in their trying times. She is a special lady.
Anna Bernotas

I met Claudette and Keely a short time ago, but they have already become a blessing. God only knows how many people have been positively impacted by them, and how many have been introduced to Jesus through their witness.
Pastor Justin Glenn

Both Keely and Claudette have been my teachers. I learned to always question Keely's behavior. Why is she unhappy? What other doctor, specialty or test do we need to access? I know all about hospitals, tests and medical conditions now as a result. Claudette's appreciation for anything, any bit of help/support shows her Christian spirit.
Heather Davis

I have known Claudette for at least 35 years. Time flies but I believe the amount of years is not as important as the benefits I have received because I know Claudette. I have seen such pure love expressed in her devotion to Keely. Claudette has courage beyond measure, determination to master the obstacles she has encountered and a faith that endures and grows. She gives full measure without complaint and loves without limits. Those that know her will agree that words will not encompass all the wonderful qualities she has in full measure and those that have never met her can be assured that words will never fully describe this remarkable woman.
Elyse Fox

There are few things in this world as beautiful as the love of a mother for a child. I have had the extreme good luck to have witnessed the love of Claudette for Keely and vice versa. It has been a rough medical road for both of them at times, and it has been a pleasure and a privilege to be involved in their care. Claudette's unconditional love for Keely has inspired me to improve my everyday empathy, compassion and giving in my medical practice and in my life.
Lori Rousche

What a joy it has been being part of both of your lives. It hasn't been long since I've cared for Keely but the depth of our relationship is so deep because of our common denominator Jesus Christ.

Keely, you have taught me in ways that I never imagined at this stage of my nursing career. You have taught me to be joyful in all circumstances and the joy of the Lord is our strength.

Claudette, you have taught me pure humility and have been the perfect example of dying to our rights, needs, and desires for ourselves. For when I look at you and experience your life in a very small way each day, I see Jesus shine through you. Jeremiah 29:11 says, "For I know the plans I have for you, declares the Lord, plans to prosper you and not to harm you, plans to give you hope and a future." You have lived this verse to its fullest. If Keely had not been born to you, she may not have gotten saved and celebrated 50 years of life on December 2008. Praise be to God for He is Lord over everything. I love you both.
Leslie Osimo

Closing thoughts . . .

My journey has been a difficult one, but it has not been without its joys. When God placed Keely in my life, it was with purpose. He chose a disabled child to draw me to Himself. For that I am filled with joy and gratitude. My walk has not been a perfect one. I am well aware of that. However, I serve a God who speaks to me of his love and forgiveness, and I have tried to extend those same qualities to those who have hurt me as well as those I have harmed. My heart is at peace. My hope is in Jesus.

Made in the USA
Charleston, SC
25 January 2010